Anderson's Guide To The Orkney Islands: With A Description

James Anderson (of Kirkwall.)

THE
KIRKWALL HOTEL.

William Dunnet, Proprietor,

BEGS to intimate that the Hotel has been recently enlarged, thus affording additional accommodation, comprising Coffee, Commercial, Billiard, and Smoking Rooms; Private Parlours, with comfortable, well aired, and spacious Bed Rooms. The Pleasure Grounds adjoining the Hotel are beautifully adorned with large trees which shade the Bowling, Croquet, and Quoit Greens. The Hotel is situated within a few minutes' walk of the Pier and in close proximity to the Cathedral and Bishop's Palace. Conveyances wait arrival of Daily Mail Steamer from Thurso.

Gentlemen staying at this Hotel may enjoy Shooting on Mr Dunnet's Farm, and Fishing in the vicinity, FREE OF CHARGE.

POSTING IN ALL ITS DEPARTMENTS.

VISITORS TO KIRKWALL

SHOULD SECURE APARTMENTS AT

Forbes' Temperance Hotel,

VICTORIA STREET.

EXCELLENT ACCOMMODATION FOR TOURISTS AND COMMERCIAL GENTLEMEN.

CHARGES MODERATE.

SHOOTING AND FISHING IN THE NEIGHBOURHOOD.

THE ROYAL HOTEL,

Victoria Street,

KIRKWALL.

JAMES SMITH

(Late Chief Steward on board the North of Scotland and Orkney and Shetland Company's Steamers)

BEGS to intimate to Commercial Gentlemen, Tourists, Sportsmen, Private Families, and the general public, that he has leased those superior, commodious, and centrally situated premises, long known as GARRICK'S HOTEL, which he will carry on in future under the name of the ROYAL HOTEL, and he trusts that by careful attention to business, and studying the requirements of his Patrons, he will merit a share of public support.

The premises have recently undergone extensive additions and improvements, are large and well furnished, containing Commercial, Coffee, Private, and Bath Rooms, numerous well aired Bedrooms, Garden, &c., and are in every way adapted to the comfort of visitors.

POSTING IN ALL ITS BRANCHES.

Fishing and Shooting.

PLEASURE BOATS FOR HIRE.

Wines, Brandies, Spirits, Ales, Porters, &c., of the Finest Qualities, in prime condition.

Machine and Boots from the Hotel in attendance at Kirkwall and Scapa Piers on arrival and departure of all steamers.

CHARGES STRICTLY MODERATE.

S.

Bells

E.

B

B E
astoni

I

In bea
the " (

Of the

B L A

I

JAM

ANDERSON'S GUIDE

TO THE

ORKNEY ISLANDS.

WITH A DESCRIPTION, BY SIR HENRY DRYDEN, BART.,

OF

The Ruined Churches in Orkney, the Bells of St. Magnus,

ETC., ETC.

KIRKWALL:
JAMES ANDERSON, "ORCADIAN" OFFICE.
EDINBURGH:
JOHN MENZIES & Co., HANOVER STREET.

KIRKWALL: PRINTED AT THE "ORCADIAN   OFFICE.

PREFACE.

THE present work is the result of complying with numerous solicitations made to the publisher by gentlemen taking much interest in the history, the antiquities, and the resources of the Orkney Islands. The files of the *Orcadian*, which newspaper has always been identified with the antiquities of the islands, presented ample materials for the purpose, and when it is stated that these materials were from the pens of such distinguished writers and authorities on the subjects of which they treated, as Sir Henry Dryden, Bart., the late James Farrer, M.P., and the late George Petrie, the well-known local archæologist, the value and accuracy of the work will be acknowledged. The materials, indeed, were sufficient for writing not merely a small hand-book, but a series of elaborate volumes, which however would not answer the purpose aimed at ; and the difficulty experienced, therefore, in preparing this Guide, was so to arrange and condense the subject matter as to form a really handy and readable work, and at the same time give a trustworthy, though brief sketch of the ancient remains, the remarkable events and customs, the magnificent scenery, and general outlines of these islands, and how they may be visited.

— Acknowledgment is here tendered to Sir Henry Dryden, Bart., for kindly revising his description of the Ruined Churches in Orkney, and his notes on the Bells of St Magnus, that appear in the appendix to the work ; to the Society of Antiquaries of Scotland, for permission to reproduce some of the wood cuts that have appeared in its transactions ; and to Mr J. W. Cursiter, F.S.A.S., who readily gave access to peruse his library of the Proceedings of the Society.

The illustrations of local objects have been engraved, and the map lithographed, specially for this work.

JAMES ANDERSON.

Orcadian Office,
Kirkwall, August, 1884.

CONTENTS.

APPENDICES.

APPENDIX A.

◆●◆

LIST OF ILLUSTRATIONS.

◆●◆

ANDERSON'S GUIDE

TO THE

Orkney Islands.

> " Restless seas
> Howl round the storm-swept Orcades ;
> Where erst St Clair bore princely sway
> O'er isle and islet, strait and bay :—
> Still nods their palace to its fall,
> Thy pride and sorrow, fair Kirkwall."

INTRODUCTION.

A HALO of romance hangs around the Orkney Islands. On every hand may be found material for the historian, the poet, the antiquary, the naturalist, and the novelist. Indeed, much that is

> . . . . . " Wild and wonderful
> In these rude isles might fancy cull ;
> For thither came, in times afar,
> Stern Lochlin's sons of roving war,
> The Norsemen, train'd to spoil and blood,
> Skill'd to prepare the raven's food,
> Kings of the main their leaders brave,
> Their barks the dragons of the wave.
> And there, in many a stormy vale,
> The Scald had told his wondrous tale ;
> And many a Runic column high,
> Had witness'd grim idolatry."

The remains of the habitations of the people of pre-historic times stand before us, silent monuments of the presence of a race of whom nothing definite can now be traced. We see their abodes (which have been left behind like " footprints on the sands of time,") we study them—our wonder and admiration are called forth, but all tradition regarding the people have gone down into the abysses of oblivion, and their surroundings, as well as their mode of living, will always remain a mystery, and at best can only be guessed at. No such mystery, however, surrounds the hardy Norsemen and Vikings who succeeded them, and whose thrilling exploits have been recorded and sung in the *Sagas*. These bold spirits, whose love of conquest fired them with an enthusiasm and daring, and an utter disregard of life, which made them a cause of fear and dread to the people of England, Ireland, and Scotland, upon whom they were continually making raids from their island homes ! In these bygone days every bay had its history, every headland its tradition, every harbour its story of rendezvous and preparation, of youthful mind stirred, of youthful ambition fired, of armaments fitted out, of seasons spent in the pursuits of war and plunder. These were also the times when the caves and the voes rang with loudly expressed joy and exultation over some more than ordinarily successful expedi- tion. But, alas ! there were also times when shattered vessels came back to tell of disaster and death; times when the wail of the widowed wife, and the bitter cries of the heart-broken mother and her children, mingled and joined in sad chorus with the wind and waves, as they dashed in upon the rock-bound shores of the lost warriors' homes.

But how, the tourist may ask, are we to get to the land of the Vikings? The routes are many and attractive. If Londoners wish to have fresh and invigorating breezes, they can make the whole journey by sea. The Edinburgh, the Leith, and the Aberdeen Steam Navigation Companies have each powerful and commodious steamers that leave London every Wednesday and Saturday, reaching Leith and Aberdeen in time to catch the North of Scotland and Orkney and Shetland Steam Navigation Company's steamers, by which pas- sengers can proceed direct to Orkney. By this route the journey will occupy about fifty hours. Or, if the west route is preferred, the Messrs Langlands despatch a steamer every Saturday from Trafalgar

Dock, Liverpool, for Stromness (Orkney.) The sea journey by this route will occupy about sixty hours. If travelling by rail is preferred, the tourist can leave the London L. & N. W. Station any evening at 8.50, or the London Great Northern at 8.30, and will reach Thurso next night about 8 o'clock, in time to catch the Orkney mail steamer at Scrabster (Thurso.) The sail across the Pentland Firth will occupy about three hours. But perhaps the best route of all is to take train to Leith or Aberdeen, and make the rest of the journey by the fine steamers of the North of Scotland and Orkney and Shetland Steam Navigation Company. From Leith to Kirkwall the journey occupies about twenty-four hours, and from Aberdeen about twelve.

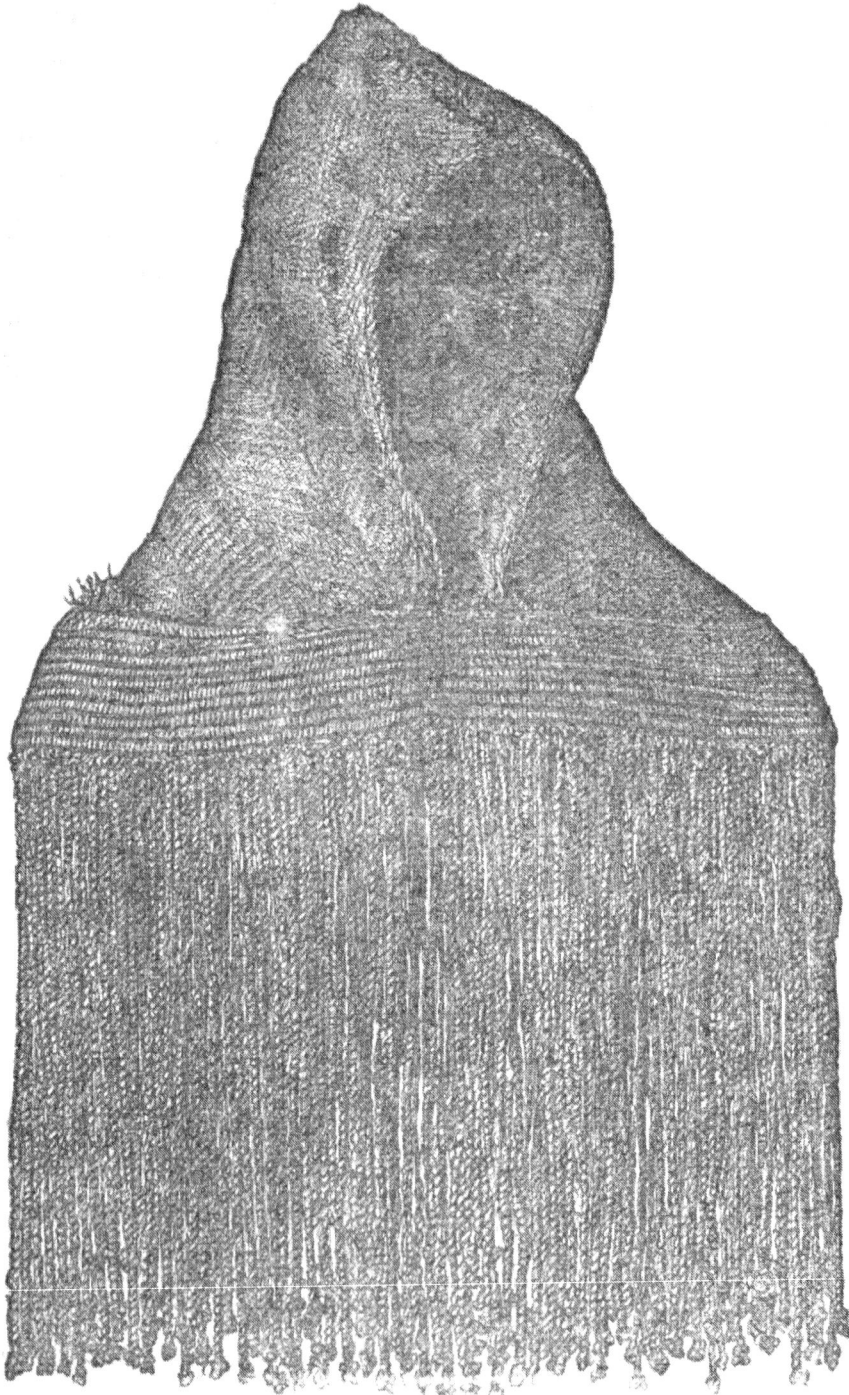

Woollen Hood, found in the Moss in the Parish of St Andrews. It is 32 inches long, 17 inches broad, and the fringe, which is of two-ply cord, is 35 inches deep. (The woodcut is inserted by the favour of the Society of Antiquaries of Scotland.)

HISTORICAL SKETCH.

"Land of the dark—the Runic rhyme—
The mystic ring—the cavern hoar ;
The Scandinavian seer—sublime
In legendary lore :
Land of a thousand Sea-kings' graves—
Those tameless spirits of the past,
Fierce as their subject Arctic waves,
Or hyperborean blast ;
Though polar billows round thee foam,
I love thee ! Thou wert once my home."

THE history of the islands may be divided into three periods—
the Pictish, the Norse, and the British.   Of the first or

The Pictish Period

There are of course no records to tell us whence these early inhabitants
came, and when they died out or left the islands ; yet they have left
behind them many monuments of their presence. Pictish brochs, houses,
and mounds are to be found in all parts of the islands ; and these, with
the standing stones and circles, will be found fully described in the
districts in which they are located, in another part of the work.
Regarding the period when the brochs were erected, there is great
difference of opinion ; but in all probability they date as far back as
the fifth or sixth century. That their inhabitants, the Picts, laid
claim to some sort of civilization is proved by the specimens of their
handiwork which have from time to time been discovered in Orkney.
These consist of hand-mills or querns, "stone whorls used in
connection with the distaff," long-handled bone combs, and stone
lamps. They had also their domesticated animals, as is shown by
the remains of cattle, sheep, and swine, which have been found.
Christianity must have been introduced into the islands in very

remote times, as is evidenced by the Ogham-inscribed stones which the antiquary has unearthed within recent years ; but it could only have flickered for a few years, and then died out, as in the ninth century the early inhabitants " were conquered, if not exterminated, by the Scandinavian worshippers of Odin and Thor."

The Norse Period

Takes its date from that time.   About the year 870, Harold Harfager, or the Fair-Haired, got up a little war on his own account, and was so successful that he managed to raise himself to the proud title of King of Norway.   This caused great discontent amongst the princes and people of Norway, with the result that they left their native country in large bodies, and swarmed the Faroes, Iceland, the Hebrides, Zetland, and the Orkney Isles—the inhabitants of the latter, it is supposed, being exterminated by the new-comers, or by Harold and his followers, who afterwards visited the islands to put a stop to the marauding excursions of the people whom, by his own bad conduct, he had forced to search for a home elsewhere.   In the *Orkneyinga Saga*, may be found a full account of the doings of the Norwegian Jarls or Earls who held sway in Orkney. These rulers had a prompt though not a very humane way of settling things.   Take one instance.   During the reign of Sigurd the Stout, who came into the Earldom about the year 980, Christianity was once more introduced into Orkney.   It seems that Olaf Tryggvi's son, then King of Norway, captured Sigurd at South Walls, and told the latter that he and his people had either to embrace Christianity and get baptised on the spot, or Hundi, Sigurd's son, would be slain.   As might be expected, Christianity was accepted as the preferable alternative ; but we are afraid the new faith only survived for a short time, for not long afterwards Sigurd fought with the heathen against the Christians in the battle of Clontarf.   With the Jarls or Earls came the Vikings, who seem to have led rather a free-and-easy kind of life.   In the summer time they left their homes to the care of those who were unfitted for battle, and with their fighting men went on marauding excursions to the adjacent coasts of Britain and

Ireland. In the autumn they returned laden with booty, upon
which they feasted and made merry during the long winter months
—sometimes slaying each other by way of a little variety. By and
bye, however, the tables turned. The Norse Jarls died out, and the
Earldom came into the possession of Scotsmen—the Angus's, the
Strathernes and the St Clairs. At this period Orkney began to be
largely peopled with the Scots, and in 1460, and 1461 the Orcadians
made bitter complaints to King Christian I., of Norway, of the raids
that were being made upon them by the "ferry-loupers"—a term
which even to the present day is applied to all who cross the Pentland
Firth, and take up their abode in "the land of the Runic Rhyme."
We now come to

The British Epoch.

While the Scotch Earls were in power, the "Annual of Norway," an
annual tribute of a hundred marks, was not paid very regularly; in fact,
during the reign of the last of the St Clair Earls, the arrears and fines had
accumulated to such an extent that, when Christian the First, King of
Denmark, Sweden, and Norway, demanded payment, the matter was
remitted to Charles, King of France, for arbitration. That Monarch
suggested, as an easy means of getting over the difficulty, the marriage
of the young Prince of Scotland and the Princess of Denmark. In 1468
an arrangement of this kind was made, a portion of 60,000 florins
being given with the Princess Margaret. Only 2000 florins were
paid at the time, however, and Orkney was given in pledge for
50,000 and Shetland for the other 8000. Two years later, King
James purchased the Earl's *hail richt* to the islands, and they were
formally annexed to the Scottish Crown by Acts of Parliament.
That was in 1470, but in 1530 the islands were granted to James
Earl of Moray, and during the rest of the century, as they were
bestowed upon one favourite of the Crown after the other, the poor
Orcadians began to know to what extent oppression could be carried.
In 1600 Earl Patrick Stewart obtained a grant of the islands, and
practised every species of exaction and oppression.. His father,
when in possession, had been bad, but the son improved upon him.

The natives were forced to build a palace for him near the Cathedral, the pundlers and bismars—old Norwegian weights—were tampered with to such an extent, that the people, who had to pay Earl Patrick in kind, found they were being charged more than the land could produce, and had to hand over their property to the oppressor. At length the cry of the oppressed reached the royal ears, and Earl Patrick ended his infamous career on the scaffold, in 1615. But the Crown, whilst punishing the thief, stuck to the stolen lands—so that virtually the complainants got no redress. Shortly after this Sir James Stewart, of Kilsyth, and Sir George Hay, of Kinfauns, held the islands as farmers-general ; but in both cases they were given up in a few years. In 1643, however, King Charles I. granted them to William Earl of Morton in mortgage, redeemable by the Crown for £30,000. Cromwell by and bye took back the lands ; but at the Restoration the Mortons regained the islands, and held them till 1669, when they were once more annexed by the Crown. Different people held leases of the islands up to 1707, when the Mortons once more secured them in mortgage, redeemable for £30,000, and subject to £500 of annual feu duty. In 1742 this grant was made irredeemable, and £7200 was received for heritable jurisdictions. In 1766, however, Sir Lawrence Dundas purchased the estate from the Mortons for £60,000 and the Earldom still remains the property of that family.

Situation and Extent of the Islands.

Before proceeding to our more immediate task, it may be well to give some general information regarding the Orkney Islands, which, we may here state, are situated off the north coast of Scotland, are separated from Caithness by the Pentland Firth, and are fifty-six in number, of which, however, only twenty-nine are inhabited. According to Captain F. W. L. Thomas, R.N., the Islands extend between the parallels 59 d. 23 m. 2 s., and 58 d. 41 m. 24 s. N. lat., and between 2 d. 22 m. 2 s and 3 d. 25 m. 10 s. W. long., and their extreme length is 41 m. 38 s., or as many geographical miles, and their breadth 1 d. 3 m. 8 s., which is equal to 32.4 geographical miles. This includes an area of 1347.8 miles, but the islands only contain 244.8 geographical miles, and their outline is equal to 573.7 miles. The islands are divided into eighteen parishes, and at last census, in 1881, the population was 32,037; in 1801 the population was 24,445.

The Climate.

Visitors to Orkney, whose stay extends over the winter, will be surprised at the equality of the temperature. Owing to the action of the Gulf Stream, which runs to Orkney, there is never a long continuance of frost or snow during the winter months, whilst in summer there is an entire absence of that sultry fatiguing heat, which is so much felt further south. Dr Clouston, the venerable minister of Sandwick, who has made meteorology a life-long study, writing on this subject says that "the mean annual temperature of Orkney is equal to that on the southern border of Scotland, but much more equable, neither so hot in summer, nor so cold in winter; that the mean annual quantity of rain is 36.95 inches, probably near the average of Scotland; the winds from the S. and W., and neighbouring points, prevail much more than from the opposite quarters, and probably tend much to promote the mildness of the climate, but this is ascribed principally to the surrounding ocean, the mean temperature of which is more than 3 deg. above that of the air, and much more in winter, so that it greatly elevates the temperature then, and depresses a little that of summer." One thing that must strike every visitor is that, in the month of June, there may be said to be no night in Orkney. At the midnight hour the smallest print may be read, whilst the songs of the birds seem never to cease, day or night. In winter, however, the Orcadian day only numbers six hours. The same eminent authority, writing on storms, says :—" If the tourist has the good fortune to be in Orkney during a storm, he will cease to regret the absence of some of the softer and more common beauties of landscape, in the contemplation of the most sublime spectacle which he ever witnessed. By repairing at such a time to the weather shore, particularly if it be on the west side of the country, he will behold waves, of the magnitude and force of which he could not have previously formed any adequate conception, tumbling across the Atlantic like monsters of the deep, their heads erect, their manes streaming in the wind, roaring and foaming as with rage, till each discharges such a Niagara flood against the opposing precipices as makes the rocks tremble to their foundations, while the sheets of water that immediately ascend, as if from artillery, hundreds of feet above their summits, deluge the surrounding country, and fall like showers on the opposite side of the island. All the springs within a mile of the weather coast are rendered brackish for some days after such a storm. Those living half a mile from the precipice declare that the earthen floors of their cots are shaken by the concussion of the waves. Rocks that two or three men could not lift are washed about, even on the tops of cliffs which are between 60 and 100 feet above the surface of the sea when smooth, and detached masses of rock of an enormous size are well known to have been carried a considerable distance between low and high water mark. Having visited the west crags some days after a recent storm, the writer found sea insects abundant on the hills near them, though about 100 feet high ; and a solitary limpet, which is proverbial for its strong attachment to its native rock, but which also seemed on this occasion to have been thrown up, was discovered adhering to the top of the cliff, seventy feet above its usual position: We apprehend it is with limpets as with ourselves, that the highest, and particularly those who are thus suddenly elevated, are not the most happy. The agitation of the sea is not always in proportion to the force of the wind, for it is sometimes very great in a perfect calm. This great swell, or *sea*, as it is here called, generally indicates a storm at a distant part of the ocean, which may reach Orkney a day or two afterwards ; hence, on the west coast, this great swell is considered a prognostic of west wind. From this we infer, 1st, that the agitation caused by the wind on the surface of the ocean travels faster than the wind itself ; and, 2d, that the breeze begins to windward, and takes some time to reach the point towards which it proceeds to leeward. Sometimes, however, the distant storm which causes this agitation does not reach these islands at all. In confirmation of this, we take the liberty of copying the following note from a register of the weather, which has for some years been kept by a clergyman on the west coast of the Mainland :—' In August 1831, from the 9th to the 13th inclusive, the great swell of the sea is remarked, every day being also marked calm. The barometer remarkably steady at 29.9, and the thermometer ranging from 55 d. to 65 d.' In a subsequent note he adds :—' On the 7th and 8th of August, there was a gale in latitude 57 d. 21 m. N., longitude 13 d. 15 m. W., at first W. by N., and afterwards S.W., as appears from a vessel damaged by it, and put back to Stromness to repair. This accounts for the great swell of the sea here from the 9th to the 13th, with calm weather. On the 11th, at one A.M., it began at Barbadoes, N.E. to N.W., and continued till seven A.M. with dreadful violence, when it had changed to S.W., E.S.E., and S. On the 11th, at four A.M., it visited St Lucie.' Many similar instances might be given where the swell was either a precursor of west wind, or marked a gale which agitated the sea to the westward."

Agriculture, &c.

The history of agriculture in the Orkney Islands has been a chequered one. One thing after another seems to have clogged the wheels of progress. In remote times the lands were held on such terms that it was impossible agriculture could make progress. If the odallers thought fit to sell their estates, their heirs, generations afterwards, could, if they chose, come in and take back the land at the same figure which their great-grandfathers may have sold it at. There was thus no encouragement for improvement. In later times, progress was barred by other obstacles. Good prices could be got for kelp, and the landlords forced their tenants to manufacture it largely. In this way the land was neglected, and when at last the price of kelp became so low that it was scarcely worth making, not a few of the Orkney landlords found themselves on the verge of bankruptcy. Orcadians all stuck tenaciously to the *run-rig* system, and those who took an active part in squaring off the land properly, were, for a time, bitterly hated by the people. Old customs died hard. For a long time farmers grew oats and bere alternately, and held out strongly against the five shift rotation. This, however, has been generally adopted, whilst fencing and draining have been extensively gone into, with the result that there is a great improvement in the crops. In fact, we doubt much whether another county in Scotland has made so much progress agriculturally, during the past thirty years, as Orkney has done. But every year farmers seem to be realising the fact that Orkney is better fitted for cattle rearing than for crop-raising; and agriculturists show a laudable zeal in improving the breed of their stock—large numbers of young pure-bred animals being brought into the county annually for breeding purposes. We may add that during the past few years new and commodious farm steadings have been rapidly taking the place of the old—and all newest improvements have been added. Specimens of the old houses, with their fire-places in the centre of the floor, and a hole in the roof for a chimney, are, however, yet to be found throughout the islands.*

Fishing.

During recent years the herring and cod fisheries, which had been on the decline, have considerably increased—better boats and material being used. A drawback to fishing in Orkney has always been that it was mainly carried on by men who were half farmers and half fishermen, and who only prosecuted the latter when their agricultural operations permitted. The want of suitable decked boats and material prevented the fishermen from searching for the fish when they had the opportunity, and it was only when shoals of herrings came close to the shore that they were successful. In 1837 the herring boats belonging to Orkney numbered 724, and the total quantity of herrings cured was 42,073 barrels, but after that the fishing declined, and in 1864 238 boats caught only 4,325 crans. In 1879 the catch was 8,418 crans for 183 boats; but since that year the example of Banffshire fishermen and others who came to Orkney, and were invariably successful, has stimulated the native crews; and with large decked boats finely equipped, the fishing gradually

* For Agricultural Statistics, see Appendix C.

increased till last year, when 205 boats had no less than 36,903 crans of fish, or an average of 180. The cod fishing, too, has considerably improved.

Anglers always find abundant sport in the numerous lochs and burns. A list of these, with relative particulars as to the time and permission to fish, will be found in Appendix F.

Linen Manufacture and Straw Plaiting, &c.

About the middle of the last century flax was grown in the islands; and linen yarn and linen itself were also manufactured; but this industry has long been given up.

In 1805 straw plaiting for ladies' bonnets was introduced, and gave large employment to the females in the islands—as many as 7000 being at one time engaged in it. When, however, the duty on foreign straw plait was reduced, the competition became too keen, and the industry succumbed. But this, as well as the destruction of the trade in kelp, was really "a blessing in disguise." When the making of kelp became unprofitable, the people were forced to devote more attention to the land; and when straw-plaiting was given up, farmers' wives and daughters turned their attention to a more congenial and more profitable employment—the rearing of poultry. That they have been successful may be judged from the fact that the value of eggs exported last year (1883) was estimated at considerably over £30,000.

Superstitions.

Like all other counties in Scotland, Orkney has had its witches, and not a few unfortunate old women have been condemned, by the superstitions of the times, to end their days at the burning stake. A case of this kind we give in Appendix B., and the curious in those matters can have their tastes further satiated by consulting the first volume of the *Abbotsford Club Miscellanies*. Where there was so much superstition, charms followed as a natural consequence. For a small consideration seamen could procure charms to bring them favouring breezes; farmers could get charms for killing the sparrows that spoiled their grain; householders could get

charms to expel rats and mice from their premises ; and charms
for bringing good luck, curing cattle, &c., were largely resorted to.
Even in the present day people have not quite lost their faith in
charms—a common enough belief being that a potato, carried
constantly on the person, will speedily cure rheumatism.

KIRKWALL BURGH ARMS (MODERN.)

THE BURGH OF KIRKWALL

WE come now to Kirkwall, which Sir Walter Scott is credited with having described as

> ' A base little burgh, both dirty and mean,
> Where there's nothing to hear, and naught to be seen,
> Save a church where of old time a prelate harangued,
> And a palace that was built by an Earl who was hanged!"

Anticipating that the tourist will make Kirkwall his head-quarters, we will first describe the town, after which we will arrange the various excursions to other parts of the mainland and islands in such a way as, we hope, will make it easy to pay a visit to every place worth seeing, with the least possible outlay and loss of time.

Kirkwall, the county town, is of great antiquity, and was probably selected as a place of residence on account of its central situation with regard to the North and South Isles, as well as its safe and commodious bay. The parish of St Ola, in which the burgh is situated, takes its name from St Olaf, second King of Norway of that name, who died in battle, 1033. Even before the Norwegian invasion of the Islands a Culdee Church stood close by the shore of the bay, and the name of Papdale, an estate near Kirkwall, leaves little doubt that a Settlement of Culdees or Irish Missionaries existed in its vicinity. It was that Church which suggested to the Norwegians the name which the town still bears in a somewhat altered form. There is no evidence that Kirkwall ever occupied more space than at present On the contrary, it has enlarged its boundaries during the present century ; but it was in former times of greater importance and exercised a widely extended influence. From about the middle

KIRKWALL, FROM THE WEST.

of the twelfth century, when it became the principal residence of the
Jarls and Bishops of Orkney and Zetland, and Jarl Rognvald founded
its Cathedral, Kirkwall continued through several centuries to be a
rendezvous of the Norwegian fleets, and the head-quarters of the fiery
Norse Jarls of Orkney, and their haughty successors of the houses of
Athole, Angus, Strathern, and St Clair.   The inhabitants of Kirkwall
in the days of the Jarls must have witnessed many a stirring scene, when
fleets of long war galleys, often gaily ornamented and crowded with
warriors, frequented the broad waters of the well-sheltered bay.
The Islands were mortgaged in 1468 to the Scottish Crown, by
Christian King of Denmark, and in 1486 King James III. erected
Kirkwall into a Royal Burgh, and conveyed by Charter to "the
Provost, Bailies, Council, and community, thereof, for the Burgh's
behoof, certain scat lands, houses, &c., particularly two crofts called
St Katherines Quoys, the Ness called Carness, the Holm of Thieves-
holm, the Crofts of Rowisquoy, Butquoy, and Quoyangry, the hill
called Kirkwall Hill, the croft called Quoybanks, the crofts of Glaitness,
Soulisquoy, Middesquoy, Pickaquoy, and Andersquoy, the hill of
Wytford and Ness of Quanterness, together with St Magnus Kirk
and all other kirks, chapels, and right of patronage within the Burgh,
and all and sundry prebendaries, teinds, and others thereto belonging,
and particularly the prebendary of St John, and all and sundry lands,
mills, farms, teinds, and teind sheaves thereof;" "and these to be
always employed and bestowed upon repairing and upholding the
said Kirk called St Magnus Kirk."   The Charter was confirmed by
King James V. in 1536, but it is questionable whether the Burgh at
any time possessed the whole of the lands and others contained in its
charters; for, in the contract made between King James VI. and
Bishop Law, in 1614, on the forfeiture of Earl Patrick Stewart, the
King disponed to the Bishop of Orkney the lands of Quoybanks,
Glaitness, and Butquoy, which had previously been conveyed to the
Burgh by the Royal Charters of James III. and James V. The
probability is that Earl Patrick or some other of the Crown Donatories
had taken violent possession of the Burgh property; but Bishop
Law was too anxious to obtain as much as possible of the new

C

domains of the Bishopric in the vicinity of Kirkwall, to be very scrupulous about the manner in which the Earls or the Crown's Lessees had come into possession of them. The teind sheaves and other teinds, parsonage and vicarage, and other kirk duties enumerated in the contract, were conveyed to the Bishop and his successors with the provision that they "should plant the kirks within the Bishoprick with ministers to serve the cure thereat with a sufficient maintenance for their stipend." In 1661, King Charles II. granted a Charter to the Burgh of Kirkwall confirming the two former charters and all other grants in favour of the Burgh, and infeftment followed on the whole in 1669. This secured to the Burgh the lands it already possessed, but it failed to restore those which had been unjustly seized and retained by the Earls and Bishops.

During the past few years the town has been much improved. It has a water and drainage scheme of which any town in Scotland might be proud, and which has cost a sum of about £14,000. A pier is in course of erection which has cost £13,000 ; and it is estimated that it will take £5,000 more to finish it ; so that the total cost will not be less than £18,000. As showing how the town has prospered of late, we may mention that the harbour dues, some thirty years ago, were let for £40 or £50 a year ; but last year the revenue of the harbour was no less than £2,000. There are some seven or eight hotels in the town, which are all fitted up with the most modern conveniences. In addition, there is a public library, a news-room, two large and commodious new schools, with a highly efficient staff of teachers, and an hospital for the sick—the latter having been bequeathed to the county by the munificence of the late Capt. John Balfour of Trenabie. But, with all these improvements, the town, when looked at from the pier, has a foreign, antiquated appearance. The houses occupy all sorts of strange positions, as if they had been thrown up in haste, and without any plan. Many of them are built with the gables facing the street. To the stranger, the town appears to be one long, narrow, circuitous street, of about a mile in length ; but branching from the principal streets, are lanes and roads leading to the suburbs, in which will be found villas of the most modern type. Commencing the exploration of the town from the pier, we enter Bridge Street, and if we peep into the second close on the left hand side, known as the " Anchor Close," we shall see the remains of an old historical building,

" The First Meeting-House of the Episcopalians in the Town of Kirkwall."

At the Revolution, towards the close of the seventeenth century, the Rev. John Wilson was one of the Episcopalian ministers of St Magnus, but was ejected by the Presbyterians. He seems, however, to have remained at Kirkwall, and when the Presbyterian minister took ill—that was in the beginning of 1703—Mr Wilson hearing there was to be no service in the Cathedral, got the town bell rung, by which the worshippers were summoned to St Magnus ; but when he was preaching to them, Mr Baikie, the Presbyterian minister, with his night-cap on, and accompanied by his wife, ascended the pulpit stairs, and turned the Episcopalian out of the pulpit. Mr Wilson, however, seems to have been pretty persevering, for we find that, on 21st February 1703, he opened an Episcopalian " meeting-house " at his residence. Portions of this building may yet be seen, as we have said, in the " Anchor Close," and some idea of the size of the tenement may be formed by the fact that it had twenty-five windows in it.

The next property on the same side of the street is occupied by the Kirkwall Hotel. It has a large open court in front, and was at one time the town residence of the Traills of Woodwick.

St Olaf Church.

A few yards further up the visitor will have no difficulty in seeing a lane, still on the same side of Bridge Street, known locally as the " Poor House Close." Upon entering this, on the left hand side, he will find an arched doorway—all that is left to give a hint of the nature of the building. Here, it is conjectured is the cite of the church from which Kirkwall took its name, and which is thought to have been erected by Rognvald Brusi's son, in memory of King Olaf the Holy; but said to have been burned early in the sixteenth century, by a party of marauding Englishmen. In the same century, however, the church was rebuilt by Bishop Reid. The whole appearance of the chapel has now been changed, and it is actually let out in tenements as a dwelling-house. A few years ago, portions of a window on the east side of the building were removed, it is said, for the purpose of being built into the new Scottish Episcopal Church. At any rate, the window is now completely built up.

Leaving this old chapel we turn into Albert Street, where the Commercial Bank occupies a commanding site. Further along we pass the Bank of Scotland on the right hand side, and the Union Bank on the left. Here the visitor will be rather amused to find a big tree in the public street, which belongs to the town, and is no doubt kept in its commanding position as a protest against the insinuation that trees will not grow in Orkney.

Kirkwall Castle.

Passing into Broad Street, on the right hand side will be seen the Castle Hotel, and on the front, which faces Castle Street, the following is inscribed :—"Near this spot, facing Broad Street, stood, in the year, 1865, the last remaining fragments of the ruins of the Castle of Kirkwall, a royal fortress of great antiquity and originally of vast strength, but of which, from the ravages of war and time, nearly every vestige had long previously disappeared. Its remains, consisting of a wall 55 feet long by 11 feet thick, and of irregular height, were removed by permission of the Earl of Zetland, on application of the Trustees acting in execution of ' The Kirkwall Harbour Act, 1859,' in order to improve the access to the Harbour; and this stone was erected to mark the cite. MDCCCLXVI." The Castle, we may add, was erected about the year 1380, by Henry St Clair, on the cite of Earl Rognvald's Castle, and was the scene of many a stirring struggle. About the beginning of the 15th century, Earl Henry II., the highly accomplished son of the first Earl Henry St Clair, lived in great pomp in it. His Court was considered to be one of the most refined in Europe, and he was surrounded by some of the proudest of Scotland's nobility, who eagerly sought admission into his service. Many names of men of rank who resided in Kirkwall about that period, and some of whom were burgesses of the burgh, are preserved in existing documents.

On the opposite side of Broad Street stood the old Orkney prison, but there is nothing left now to mark its site. Proceeding along Broad Street we pass the News-room, where the visitor may enter, and see the latest telegrams, which are received twice a-day. We have now a full view of

St Magnus Cathedral,

Which is the chief ornament of the town, and as the events that led to its erection throw a strong light upon the state of society in Orkney, in these bye-gone days, we may here give a brief outline of some of the most important of them. Towards the close of the eleventh century, Hakon, the son of Paul, and Magnus, the son of Erlend, two cousins, came upon the scene. The former appears to have had the strong love of his forebears for conquest, whilst the latter, even in his youth, seemed to have been cut out for a saint. It is related of him that when his friends were fighting in the Menai Straits, Magnus would not strike a blow, but remained on deck singing psalms. However, from the following quotation it will be seen that he sometimes fought, but from the

high character he gets, we must take it that he never fought in a
wrong cause :—" He was a man of large stature, a man of noble
presence and intellectual countenance. He was of blameless life,
victorious in battle, wise, eloquent, strong-minded, liberal, and
magnanimous, sagacious in council, and more beloved than any other
man. To wise men and good he was gentle and affable in his
conversation ; but severe and unsparing with robbers and vikings.
Many of these who had plundered the landowners and the inhabitants
of the land he caused to be put to death. He also seized murderers
and thieves, and punished rich and poor impartially for robberies
and thefts and all crimes. He was just in his judgments, and had
more respect to divine justice than difference in the estates of men.
He gave large presents to chiefs and rich men, yet the greatest
half of his liberality was given to the poor. In all things he strictly
obeyed the Divine commands ; and he chastened his body in many
things which in his glorious life were known to God, but hidden
from men." The popularity of Magnus raised the ire of his cousin
Hakon, who did not take much pains to hide his spleen, and the
natural consequence was that their friends had a good deal of
trouble in preventing an open rupture. At length Hakon got
Magnus to promise to meet him at Egilshay—stipulating that they
should only be accompanied by two boats each, with an equal body
of men. The latter kept his promise, but the former took with him
eight war-ships, and a large force. Magnus knew what all this
meant ; but instead of fighting, as his followers desired him to do,
he, to save his cousin from the guilt of bloodshed, made the following offers :—If Hakon wished, he (Magnus) would go to Rome,
and never return, or Hakon could send him to Scotland, and detain
him there, or he could cast him into a dungeon and blind or maim
him. Hakon would in all probability have accepted the last proposal,
but his followers would not ; they declared one of the Earls must
die, as they were tired of the joint rulership, and Magnus was then
ordered to be executed—16th April 1110. His executioner, Lifolf,
did not at all like the job, and showed signs of wavering. He was
thus encouraged, however, by St Magnus to strike the blow :—

" Stand before me and hew me a mighty stroke on the head, for it is not fitting that high-born lords should be put to death like thieves. Be firm, poor man, for I have prayed to God for you, that he may have mercy upon you." The *Saga* adds : — " After that he signed the sign of the Cross, and stooped under the blow, and his spirit passed into heaven." His remains were first interred at Christ Kirk, Birsay, which became a resort for pilgrims for many years. A few years later Rognvald was created Earl by King Sigurd, and was given half the Orkneys. Rognvald four years after this attempted to make good his claim, but Paul, the reigning Earl, first of all defeated Rognvald's consort, Olvir Rosta, off Tankerness, and then proceeded to Shetland, and captured Rognvald's ships. Rognvald, when he got back to Norway, began making preparations for another attack upon Orkney, and he vowed, if he were successful, he should build " a stone minster at Kirkwall," to be dedicated to his uncle, Earl Magnus. By some clever manoeuvring, Rognvald landed safely at Westray, and got his claim settled, with the aid of Bishop William, without having to strike a blow. In 1137 Rognvald proceeded to fulfil his vow, by having the foundation stone of St Magnus laid, and by forcing the people to give him the necessary coin to allow him to proceed with the work. After paying a visit to Jerusalem, Rognvald came back to Orkney, fought a few more battles, and was at last slain in Caithness, where he had gone on a hunting expedition. That was in 1158, and he was canonised in 1198. Additions were made to the Cathedral in 1350, 1511, and as late as 1540. It is difficult to point out the exact limits of Earl Rognvald's work, but unquestionably it includes the western portion of the choir, commencing with the two eastern pillars of the tower, and extending to about the centre of the great wall piers, which stand to the west of the altar steps. The style of this part of the Cathedral, as well as of the transepts, is Romanesque, and it is therefore probable that the latter were also built by Earl Rognvald. The nave, as far as the fifth pier or pillar from the western pillars of the tower, is also in the Romanesque style, but is evidently of a somewhat later date than the western portion of the choir and transepts, and hence it has been supposed to have been built by William, first Bishop of Orkney, who, as recorded in an Icelandic annal, died in the year 1168. Strangers can always get the keys of the Cathedral for the asking, and they should not lose the opportunity of going inside, where lie the remains of many distinguished persons. In 1263, Hakon King of Norway, after his disastrous defeat at Largs, came to Kirkwall, and died of a broken heart. His remains were then placed before the "shrine of St Magnus," until the spring, when they were carried across to Norway. In 1290, the Maid of Norway, daughter of King Eric of Norway, died in South Ronaldshay, and was buried within the precincts of the Cathedral. Thus within the brief space of twenty-seven years, a King of Norway and a Queen of Scotland died in Kirkwall; and yet at the present day there are many educated persons even in Scotland who have no better idea of the geographical position of a town which was once the metropolis of the North of Scotland, than, to use a vulgar phrase, that it is somewhere "at the back o' beyont." William, the first Bishop of Orkney, filled the See from at least 1112 to 1168, and was buried in the Cathedral. The Icelandic Annal narrates that "in this year (1168) died William the Old, first Bishop of Orkney." A circumstance occurred in 1848, while the Cathedral was being repaired, which was not only interesting in itself, but also corroborates the statement in the annal, and shows the historical value of the Northern Chronicles. A cist or grave, similar to those found in the barrows or Tumuli, was discovered between the first and second pillars at the east end of the north side of the choir; a skeleton lay doubled up in the cist, and beneath the chin there was stuck a flat piece of lead, on which was rudely scratched or incised, " *H. requiescit Williamus, senex felicis memorie*," and on the reverse, " *Pmus Epis.*" The annal and the inscription are thus found to agree in calling him *Senex*, or the Old, on account of the great age which he attained, and in describing him as *Primus Episcopis*, or the first Bishop (of Orkney). Rognvald, the founder of the Cathedral, also found a resting place within it, as did St Magnus, as well as numbers of Bishops and

Earls ; and round its walls are ranged many quaint memorials of the dead. The internal length of the Cathedral is 217½ feet, of which the choir (now re-seated) is 86 feet, and the nave 131½ feet. The total internal width is about 57 feet, and the width of the choir and nave between the pillars 16¾ feet. The height to the vaulting is 71 feet, and the total height to top of spire about 140 feet. The nave has 7 pillars or piers on each side, separating it from the north and south aisles, and the choir is in like manner separated from the aisles by five pillars on each side. A glance at the exterior detects such differences, both in style and the appearance of the stones used, as makes it evident that additions have been made to both ends of the buildings, and also to its original height; and that the central part, including a considerable portion of the choir, nave, and transepts, is the oldest. An inspection of the interior exhibts a marked difference in the style and workmanship even of the portion just referred to, and leads to the inference that it has been built under the superintendence of different persons. The three western bays of the choir, as far as the middle of the large square pier, the transepts, and the five eastern bays of the nave, including the five pillars on each side, immediately to the westward of the tower piers, are Romanesque. This style prevailed in Scotland until about 1170, which quite corresponds with the date assigned to this part of the building from its foundation in 1137 to the death of William the first Bishop of Orkney, in 1168. According to Professor Daniel Wilson, the first pointed style, corresponding with the early English, came into use in Scotland about 1170, and continued till 1242, and contemporaneous with it, what he names the Scottish Geometric style, which was peculiar to Scotland, and prevailed until 1285. To one or other of these styles belongs the greater part of the remainder of the Cathedral not already described. It has been generally supposed that the three eastern bays and east end of the choir is of comparatively modern date, but this portion so closely resembles, in characteristic features, other buildings which can be satisfactorily shewn to belong to the period assigned to the Geometric style, that it seemed reasonable to infer in the absence of

evidence to the contrary, that this part of the Cathedral of St
Magnus is of the same antiquity, and was probably erected between
the beginning and middle of the 13th century. While the beautiful
clustered shafts and mouldings are first pointed, the arches are
Romanesque, showing a combination of both styles, which was very
likely to occur at the period of transition from one style to the
other. The pillars of the tower arches belong probably to the same
period, and the great eastern window, with its twelve-leaved rose,
to the close of the Geometric style. The tower and western
windows are apparently of a later date, as also some of the doors.
But there is no evidence to show that there is any truth in the
opinion generally entertained that Bishop Edward Stewart built the
addition to the east end of the choir, and his successor, Bishop
Robert Reid, erected the three western pillars of the nave, about
the middle of the 16th century. On the contrary, there is the
strongest evidence in the building itself that the portions attributed
to them were erected 300 years earlier. No doubt some of the
windows and doors have been inserted, and other alterations made,
at much later dates, but the greater part of the Cathedral was built
in the 12th and 13th centuries. Perhaps the greatest difficulty
which has been encountered in attempting to ascertain the dates of the
respective additions, has arisen in overlooking the existence of the
Geometric style peculiar to Scotland, and seeking to reconcile its
distinctive characteristics with the English first pointed. A careful
comparison, however, of the Cathedral of St Magnus with the
Abbey of Aberbrothoc, founded in 1178, by William the Lion, and
with others of that period, which exhibited the same peculiarities of
the Scottish Geometric style, might furnish a satisfactory clue to the
puzzle that has hitherto baffled the skill of eminent archæologists.
There are two small figures in stone in the Cathedral in Kirkwall,
which, in the opinion of the late Professor Munch of Christiania,
who saw them in 1849, represent respectively St Olaf, King of
Norway, and St Magnus, Earl of Orkney. It has been objected
that the sword in the hand of the figure representing St Magnus is
inappropriate, because he was not of a warlike spirit ; but it must

be kept in mind, that although he refused to fight in an unjust quarrel, yet the manner in which he met his death, showed that he was no coward. Most probably the sword was intended as a symbol of rank and authority, and was no more out of place in the hand of St Magnus than the battle-axe in the hand of the figure which represents St Olaf. About the beginning of this century some stones were removed from the large pier on the north side of the choir of Kirkwall Cathedral, when a cavity was discovered containing some human bones, which were believed at the time to be the remains of St Magnus. They were restored to their resting place where they lay forgotten till they were accidentally re-discovered during the repairs on the building in 1849, when they were once more carefully deposited in the pillar. In September, 1867, the Marquis of Bute having learned, during his visit to Kirkwall, that the bones just referred to were traditionally believed to be the remains of St Magnus, requested permission to re-open the cavity in the pier of the choir and examine the remains. They were carefully taken out and minutely examined by Lord Bute, in the presence of Drs Logie and Kirkpatrick, Mr Iverach, chemist, and Mr G. Petrie. The skull was found in a fair state of preservation, but bleached very white. A lower human jawbone was found with the other bones, but it evidently did not belong to the skull beside which it lay, but to a much older person than the skull indicated. There was an indentation $1\frac{3}{8}$ inch long, $\frac{7}{8}$ of an inch broad, and about 3 sixteenths of an inch deep on the top of the skull, commencing at the point where the sagittal suture joins the coronal suture, and extending backwards. The internal surface of the skull did not appear to have been fractured by the blow which crushed in the external table or surface. The wound had not apparently been the immediate cause of death, but seemed to have been an old one, for the serrated edges of the sagittal suture were interrupted or obliterated by a new deposition of bony matter on the injured portion of the skull. There was also a distinct trace of an old sword cut on the top of the head, a little to the right of the indentation. The skull was of large dimensions, very thick and massive, and very broad across the posterior portion. The occipital protuberance was unusually prominent and sharp. The forehead was of medium height but narrow, and the small portion of the nasal bones which remained, indicated a prominent or aquiline nose. The other bones of the skeleton, especially the thigh and leg bones, were very large, and evidently belonged to a man of tall stature and great muscular development. The following measurements of the skull were taken in the presence of Lord Bute, viz:—Occipito-frontal arch from occipital protuberance to root of nose, $14\frac{1}{8}$ inches. From upper edge of ear-hole on each side over highest part of skull, $13\frac{3}{4}$ inches. Short or transverse diameter of skull at broadest part, $6\frac{1}{8}$ inches. Breadth of face, measured across it to outer edge of orbit on each side as the orbits now are (part of the outer margin on each side being broken off), $4\frac{1}{4}$ inches. The bones which were found in the pillar on 19th September, 1867, as before described, were as follows :—Cranium ; inferior maxilla ; three vertebrae ; part of os sacrum ; left malar bone ; right and left humrus ; right and left femur, $18\frac{1}{2}$ inches long ; right tibia and fibula ; left tibia ; right and left os calcis ; right and left astragulus ; one bone of great toe ; six tarsal bones, and one bone of finger. One or two fragments of an oak coffin were also found with the bones. The cavity which contained the bones was far too short for a human skeleton to lie extended at full length, and had evidently been only made for the re-interment of a skeleton which had been removed from another place. The probability therefore is that either when the Cathedral was lengthened at the east end, or at the period of the Reformation, the remains of St Magnus were deposited in the large pier, the west side of which belongs to the original structure, and the east to the addition which was subsequently made to the choir. The pier is thus a connecting link between the old and the later portions of the Cathedral, and was probably on that account selected as a fitting receptacle for the " relics " of St Magnus. The whole of the relics were after examination carefully replaced in the pillar and the cavity reclosed, but excellent photographs of the skull were previously taken by Mr William Flett, photographer, Kirkwall.

When the alterations were being carried out by the Woods and Forests Commissioners between thirty and forty years ago, a curious " find " was made. In the south aisle of the choir, just at the entrance to the portion of the building now screened, a part of the masonry which did not seem to be in keeping with the rest of the building attracted attention; and, upon a stone being removed, a skeleton was found in a niche of the wall—the head facing the west, and the feet the east. The knees were drawn up, as if the space had been too short for the body. Upon examination, it was found that a portion of the skull had been fractured. In the choir there is or was a light grey marble slab, under which Professor Traill found a skeleton, on the breast of which there was lying an iron pin with a gold head. The skeleton was supposed to be of a young female, and was put down to be that of the Maid of Norway. At the east end of the north aisle of the choir, whilst the alterations were being carried out in 1848, a slab, with the following inscription was found:—" Here Lyes Captain Patricio of the Spanish Armada, who was wrecked on the Fair Isle, 1588." The slab had evidently been brought from a distance, as it was of green freestone, and no stones of this description are to be found in Orkney. The visitor should, before leaving the Cathedral, see the alms-plates which are very large and unique. They are of Dutch workmanship, and are made of brass. The largest one is embellished with a representation of Adam and Eve, the tree, serpent, and so on, and round the edge is inscribed :—" Had Adam gedaen Gods woort wys soo vaer hy gebleven int pardys. Ano. 1636." (Had Adam obeyed God's words, so had we then lived in paradise.) The other has much the same embellishments, but no inscription. In the vestry the " mort brod " can be seen, with its curious inscriptions and ornamentations. " The Annal of Norway," to which we referred in the Historical Sketch, had yearly to be delivered into the hands of the Bishop of Orkney, within the Cathedral of St Magnus, or in his absence, it had to be deposited with the canons of the Cathedral.

We may mention another curious matter in connection with this old building. In *Wallace's Description of Orkney*, Edinburgh, 1693, p. 72, it is said " the King (Robert Bruce) after the victory (of Bannockburn) ordered that for ever after five pound sterling should be paid to *St Magnus* Kirk in *Kirkwall*, out of the customs of *Aberdeen*." If that sum was ever paid, it at any rate has long ago been discontinued. It is now well nigh a hopeless task to walk through the noble old building and point out its limits at the respective deaths of Earl Ronald and Bishop William. This arises in a great measure from the well-known practice of copying in many edifices the styles of former periods, instead of adopting the style of the age in which they were erected. It thus not unfrequently happens that, in the enlargement of ancient edifices, the additions have been made so closely to resemble the style of the original building, that even an experienced archæologist cannot with certainty distinguish the one from the other. Thus it is that in the Cathedral of St Magnus, which has been enlarged from time to time, the difference in style is not reckoned sufficient evidence by which to determine the respective dates of the additions. For example, the Romanesque arches can scarcely be taken conclusively to prove that the whole of that part of the Cathedral where they exist, was built either by Earl Ronald or Bishop William, because, while there is great probability that such was the case ; yet, on the other hand, the variety which is observable even in this apparently the oldest portion of the building, and which may only evince the variety of taste of the Earl and Bishop, may simply be the result of the copying system, attempting, in the 15th or 16th century, to imitate the style of the 12th century. We may add that St Magnus Cathedral was re-seated and repaired by the heritors at an expense of £2,000, in 1856.

Having admired the architectural and other beauties of the venerable pile, the visitor should now mount the tower, which is 133 feet high, though originally, before it was burned down, it was much higher. On the way up, the tourist will have an opportunity of testing the tone of the bells, which were supplied by Bishop Maxwell in 1525, and are said to have been cast at Edinburgh Castle by

Rothwick, master gunner of James IV.* He will also see the old gallows, which was at one time used for executing criminals at the Gallows Hall. Though the stairs to the top of the tower are dark, narrow, twisty, and dusty, the visitor will be amply rewarded for his toil by the magnificent view to be had from the eminent situation —especially if the day be clear.

The Market Cross.

Leaving the Cathedral, and crossing the space in front of it, will be found the Market Cross, which is of grey freestone, and was erected by Bishop Graham, in 1621. A few years ago the Cross was broken, but has now been clasped and placed in its original position. Every Christmas and New Year's Day the people engage in a tussel over a ball which is thrown up at the Cross, and any one who has seen the struggle must have been convinced that the Norse blood of their forefathers still courses in the veins of Kirkwallians. In former years scenes of quite a different discription were to be witnessed at the Cross. For instance, on the 22nd September, 1678, Margaret Corner, for stealing some bed linen, was sentenced to stand in the " joggs " one hour, after which she was to be scourged at the Market Cross—the lockman being ordered to give her twelve lashes and put " her af ye toun." The poor woman was also threatened with death if she was ever afterwards found stealing forty pennyworth.

New Town Hall.

Facing us in Broad Street, we have the new Town Hall, which is being erected at a cost of about £6,000, and which is to contain the Post Office, museum, and other public offices. Proceeding up Broad Street we come to

The Old Town House,

Which was built about the year 1750. It stands upon what was part of the old grave-yard, which surrounded the Cathedral. Earl Morton contributed £200 towards the building of it, and gave

* For full description of the bells see Appendix E.

permission to the Town Council "to use some of the stones of the old Castle of Kirkwall," for its erection, on condition that the Sheriff was allowed the principal hall for holding his Courts.* In past years the County Balls were held here; and the rooms of the old building rang with the mirth of Orkney's brightest sons and daughters; but its glory has departed. It has been condemned as unsuitable for the meetings of Municipal authorities—it has even been condemned as being unfit for use as a prison.

On the other side of the street is Tankerness House, a grand old building, above the doorway of which may be seen the arms of Archdeacon Fulsie and his wife. We now enter Victoria Street, and pass the National Bank on the left hand side. A little further up, and nearly opposite the Post Office, is the site on which stood the old Episcopal Palace in which King James V. of Scotland was entertained by Bishop Maxwell, in 1540. As we proceed further south, arms of private families, as well as Latin mottos, will be seen above various doorways. As we pass into Main Street, the Hospital, which, as we have already stated, was bequeathed to the county by Captain Balfour, attracts attention—being a large three-storey house, with iron railings in front. Just before turning into High Street, there is an unpretentious-looking building—the Roman Catholic Chapel—but none of its members are Orcadians. There is nothing calling for note in High Street, till we reach the extreme south end of the town, when we come in full view of the new County Poor-house, which has just been completed at a total cost of £2,500. To the right is the Glaitness School, with accommodation for 120 scholars, whilst straight in front, far southwards, we get a glimpse of South Ronaldshay. Standing here we get a full view of Glaitness, which runs up toward the west; Corse, which rises in a south-westerly direction; and Quoybanks which stretches up towards the east. These lands all belonged at one time to the Church (Quoy-banks is all that now remains of the glebe), and as a sample of how Bishops managed things in these days, we give the following quaint story from Macfarlane's MSS :—" At the Reform, and until some

* For Correspondence on this subject see Appendix D.

time after, Bishop Graham was Bishop of Orkney ; the Room of Glatness in the said parish of St Ola, which lies upon the south shore of the Oyse, and pays yearly upwards of twenty bolls of malt, was the minister's glebe. But the said Bishop Graham, looking out at his window one day, when Mr Patrick Inglis, minister of Kirkwall, and other ministers, were with him, and viewing Glatness, said, Mr Patrick, I must have that Room of Glatness from you, and I will give you the Room of Corse for it, because it lieth in mine eye; whereunto Mr Patrick, whispering the Bishop in the ear, said, D—— pick out that greedy eye, my Lord, that would take *Gladness* from me and give me *Cross*. But the Bishop accordingly did it, and after that, thinking the Room of Corse too good yet, took that away, and gave the Room of Quoy Banks, which is not in value above £3 sterling yearly, and sometimes let below it. Thus the Bishops served their brethren."

Retracing our steps as far as the Junction Road, we turn to the right into the New Scapa Road. Five minutes' walk brings us to a path that branches off to the left towards the Holm Road. Northwards from here, Kirkwall has a very catching appearance. To the south we get a splendid view of Scapa Bay, where a new pier has just been built at a cost of £14,000 ; south-west, the Hoy hills are seen looming in the distance ; westwards, we have the whole stretch of Wideford Hill ; and eastwards, on the face of the hill we are ascending, is the Highland Park Distillery. Upon reaching the Holm Road, we strike off to the left again towards the town, and a few minutes' walk brings us to Gallow Hall, so called because in olden times felons were executed here. Going straight down the hill, we have attractive villas on the right, and in the centre of the row stands the new Scotch Episcopal Chapel (St Olaf's). At the lower end of the villas—nearer the town—is the U P. Church, which, though plain, is substantial, and is one of the largest congregations of the denomination in Scotland—the membership being about 1200. Here we turn to the left, into Palace Street, and after passing the Independent Church and Manse, we have facing us the Cathedral, and the Bishop's Palace and Tower, whilst to the left, surrounded with trees, we see

D

The Earl's Palace.

" Still doth the ruined Palace stand,
  A crumbling relique in the land.—
Tenantless fabric! huge and high,
And proud in ruined majesty.
The verdant ivy robes thy wall,
Weeds are the dwellers of thy hall,
And in the wind the tufted grass
  Waves o'er thy dim and mouldering mass ;
  And freshly each returning spring
  Blooms o'er thy mortal withering.
On darkening piles and waning wrecks
    A gay green garment oft is spread ;
For ruin, as in mockery, decks
    The faded victims she hath made!

" With Time and tempest thou art bent,
  A drear neglected monument :
Lorn as some frail and aged one,
Who lives when all his friends are gone !—
Where is thy voice of music ?—Where
The strains that hushed the midnight air,
When beauty woke her witching song,
And spell-bound held the festive throng ?—
A narrow and a nameless grave
Hath closed upon the fair and brave,
And all around is deadly still,
Save when, from some high pinnacle,
The raven's croak or owlet's wail
Blends with the sighing of the gale."

This Palace was built by Patrick Stewart, Earl of Orkney, in the year 1600. A bad ruler but an excellent architect, he, in order to indulge his particular hobby, never scrupled cruelly to oppress his people, making them transport heavy masses of stone, and perform all manner of servile work, and all this without any kind of compensation. A contemporary writer gives the following life-like portrait of him, which was found by Mr Robert Chambers in the Edinburgh Privy Council Archives, and which we quote as being in all probability new to most of our readers :—" He had a princely and royal revenue, and indeed behavit himself with sic sovereignty, and gif I durst say the plain verity, rather tyrannically, by the shadow of Danish laws, different and more rigorous nor the municipal or criminal laws of the rest of Scotland, whereby no man of rent or purse might enjoy his property in Orkney without his special favour, and the same dear bought. And his pomp was so great in Kirkwall, that he never went from his Castle to the Kirk, nor abroad otherwise, without the convoy of fifty musketeers and other gentlemen of convoy and guard. And before dinner and supper there were three trumpeters that soundit till the meat of the first service was set at table, and sic like at the second service, and consequently after the grace. He also had his ships directed to the sea to intercept pirates and collect tribute of uncouth fishers that came yearly to these seas. Whereby he made sic collection of great guns and other weapons for weir (war) as no house, palace, nor castle, yea, all in Scotland were not furnished with the like. At length the deeds of this island lord became so bold, rebellious, and tyrannical that he was arrested, brought to Edinburgh, tried and sentenced to be beheaded, although he was cousin-german to King James VI., the Earl's father being a natural son of James V. So ignorant of letters was this potent Earl, that it is recorded that, when the ministers found he was unable to repeat the Lord's prayer ' they entreated that his execution might be delayed a few days till he were better informed.' This was acceded to, and when he took the sacrament, he was beheaded."

Notwithstanding this alleged ignorance on the part of Earl Patrick, however, De Foe, in his tour through Great Britain (8th edition, 12mo., London, 1778 ; vol. iv. p. 311) tells that several of the rooms of his palace were " curiously painted with Scripture stories." Even in decay, this grand old building has a magnificent appearance. The central portion is oblong, and the massive wings at the north and south ends, with the towers and oriel windows, give the whole building a palatial and castellated appearance ; whilst the trees surrounding it, the Bishop's Tower and Palace to the West of it, and the Cathedral to the north, all tend to give it a touch of the picturesque. Proceeding to the grand entrance, which is at the north-east corner of the southern wing, the visitor is at once struck with the richness of the ornamentation. There is a coronet at each side of this beautifully ornamented circular doorway, above the coronets there are two figures, and still higher up there is a white free-stone pannel, upon which the Earl's arms in all probability have been carved ; but the finger of Time has obliterated all trace of these. As we enter the Palace, we find that the various passages, and all the apartments, have got circular ceilings. We need not enter into a detailed description of each room. Suffice it to state that thirteen apartments may still be counted. A walk through the building will convince the most superficial observer that its architect had not only an eye to the beautiful, but had made every provision for the safety and comfort of its owner. The lower chambers which run round the ground floor, must have been eminently suited for the safety of those within, whilst the well at the side of the passage leading to the kitchen would give a plentiful supply of water at all times. In the spacious kitchen there is a large fire-place, which would indicate that Earl Patrick was no vegetarian. On the first landing of the principal stair there is a large aperture communicating with the kitchen, which has evidently been used for sending up the different courses to the banqueting hall. This latter room has been the chief apartment, a sort of state room, and runs from north to south along the whole central portion of the building. The windows are magnificent. Along the east side there are two large oriel windows, on the west side there is another of the same description, and at the south end there is a large Gothic window. There are two large fire-places in the room. The one at the north end has nothing specially attractive about it, and would in all probability have been pretty much hid by the gallery which seems to have been above it.

At the side of this fire-place there is a doorway which opens into the drawing-room. The other fire-place, in the west side of the room is a marvel in architecture. It is over 14 feet wide, and has a horizontal lintel of blocks of free-stone, cut and neatly jointed together so as to have the appearance of an arch, but the effect of one solid stone, and never fails to attract the attention of architects, who are unanimous in bestowing the greatest praises upon it as a work of art. At each side of the fire-place are pillars, which are surmounted by coronets, and on the bands under the coronets can be deciphered the initials—P.E.O. (Patrick Earl of Orkney.) The other apartment to which we would direct special attention is the chapel, which is richly ornamented, and in which a piscina may still be seen. If we go outside, and closely examine the balcony windows, we cannot but admire the variety of styles adopted—some being square, others octagonal, and others again are circular. But

> "The statliest mansion man can raise
> Is the ivy's food at last,"

And the Earl's Palace is no exception to this rule, as it is going fast to ruin. *Sic transit gloria mundi.*

On the same grounds the County Buildings and Prison have lately been erected; but they look tawdry when compared with the adjoining palace. We leave the Palace Grounds at the south-west, and enter the Water Gate, where, according to MacFarlane's account of Kirkwall (1726), on the south end of the Bishop's Palace, "and within the area and iron gates, was the minister's manse, a long house well lighted with sufficient rooms; the same is also now ruinous and the occasion of its going to ruin was this: In the days of Cromwell's usurpation, there being an English garrison in Orkney, the Governor and principal persons resided at Kirkwall. Mr James Douglas being then Minister of Kirkwall, and living in the said manse, Governor Watson, for so was he called, desired of the minister the favour of his manse for a lodging, because it lay conveniently for him, being within the gates of the Palace, promising to pay forty-eight pounds Scots money yearly, and to leave it to him in as good condition when he should be called off. The Session Records of Kirkwall bear, that the said Governor did pay according to promise punctually when required. But Mr Douglas, being suspended for countenancing Montrose, who was then under sentence of excommunication, when the Governor, on the restoration of King Charless II., went off, and so, not having title to the manse, did not seek to re-enter it, by which means it went somewhat to decay; and when, upon the introduction of Episcopacy, and Mr Douglas his conforming thereto, he would have returned, he could not until it should be repaired. The town refused to repair it, because it was not within their precincts, and the Bishop refused to do it, because it was the manse of the minister of the town; but, in a session at Kirkwall, where Bishop Honeyman was present with the Magistrates, they agreed that the Bishop pay yearly twenty-four pounds Scots in lieu of house-mails, and the town as much, making in whole forty-eight pounds money foresaid, aye and while the manse should be repaired by those who should be found liable in law to repair it; and from that time to this present the town's part, being twenty-four pounds Scots, hath been and is paid yearly out of the kirk-treasury of the Session of Kirkwall. The bishop's part also was paid by Bishop Honeyman and Bishop M'Kenzie, until the said Bishop M'Kenzie's last year, an. 1687; but, since the Revolution, the said minister of Kirkwall never got any thing out of the bishoprick on that account." This is one of the buildings the Crown took from the town, and which caused a good deal of justified grumbling. Proceeding a few yards northwards along the Water Gate, we reach

The Bishop's Palace.

" And thy heart sank, Haco, Haco,
    And though thou felt that thou must die,
When the bay of Kirkwall, Haco,
    Thou beheld with drooping eye.

" And they led thee. Haco, Haco,
    To the bishop's lordly hall,
Where thy woe-struck barons, Haco,
    Stood to see the mighty fall."

It is situated a few yards to the south of the Cathedral. The Romanesque arches, and general appearance of the older part of the ruins of the Bishop's Palace, anciently called " the Place of the

THE BISHOP'S PALACE.

Yairdis," exhibit a striking resemblance to the portion of the Cathedral attributed to Bishop William. There is, therefore, good reason to believe, that these ruins include the remains of the residence built 700 years ago by him, when he removed his residence from

Egilsey to Kirkwall. At all events, we know that the " Place of the Yairdis" was in existence in 1263, or less than 100 years after his death. It was in this Palace that King Hacon died. The story of this monarch's latter days is easily told.

In the year 1263, Alexander III., King of Scotland, determined to make a strenuous effort to expel the Norwegians from the Hebrides, and annex the islands to his own dominions. Intelligence of his designs was conveyed to Hacon, King of Norway, who forthwith equipped a large fleet, and sailed for Scotland ; being noways disposed to surrender, without a struggle, so large a territory, which Scandinavian prowess had acquired, and so long possessed. Gilbert, Earl of Orkney, was at that time in Norway, and accompanied Hacon in his expedition, The fleet, having called at Shetland, proceeded to Orkney, and cast anchor in the Bay of Elwick, in Shapinsay, which must have presented a very picturesque and animated appearance when crowded with the Norwegian ships. After a short stay, Hacon went with his fleet to the island of South Ronaldshay, and, having remained there for some time, once more put to sea and steered for the Hebrides, where at first he was victorious. But winter setting in, many of his ships were wrecked ; and having been defeated by the Scots in the battle of Largs, he was compelled to return to Orkney with his shattered fleet and dispirited followers. The return of Hacon presented a striking contrast to his brief visit a month or two previously. He and his followers were then elated with the hope of victory, and embarked amid every demonstration of boisterous joy. But they returned greatly thinned in their ranks, disappointed in their hopes and ambition, and smarting under the shame of unexpected defeat. Their landing at Scapa Bay was effected amid gloom and silence, very different from the joyous welcome that they once anticipated. The Norwegian fleet must have been a very numerous one when Hacon started on his ill-fated expedition, for, besides the ships lost in the Hebrides, and a considerable number subsequently despatched to Norway, he retained twenty ships in Orkney, where he resolved to spend the winter, being deterred from proceeding to Norway by a prevalence of stormy weather, which rendered the passage extremely dangerous at that season.

Worn out by the fatigue, anxiety, and disappointment consequent on the summer's campaign, the King, immediately on his arrival in Kirkwall, was confined to bed in the Bishop's Palace. In a few days he rallied so far as to be able to walk about in his apartments, and next day attended Mass in the Bishop's chapel. The following day the old warrior King went across to the Cathedral, and walked round the shrine of "St Magnus" in the vain hope that his failing strength would be restored through the intercourse of the canonized Earl. But the flickering flame of life now sank lower in its socket, and Hacon returned to his bed in the palace, from which he was never again to rise. At one time he caused the chronicles of his predecessors on the throne of Norway to be read to him, and at another the legends of the Romish Saints. At last finding that death was at hand, he wrote to his son, and summoned to his bedside the nobles and Bishops who had accompanied him on his ill-fated expedition, and gave them his parting instructions. He then directed that certain sums should be distributed among his courtiers and servants, and that if there was not a sufficient amount in his treasurer's hands, his plate should be taken to make it up. Hacon's death took place here in the Bishop's Palace, on the 16th December 1263, and his body was carried to an upper apartment where it lay in state for some time, and was then removed to the Cathedral, and placed before the shrine of the patron Saint, surrounded with great pomp, and remained there all winter watched by the nobles. In April, the coffins containing the remains of King Hacon were taken to Scapa, and conveyed in the Admiral's galley to Norway.

Connected with the tower of the Bishop's Palace, an archway crossed the road, but a few years ago it was considered to be so dangerous that it was removed, and built into the east wall of the old building. On the north western side of the tower is a pannel, on which may be seen the Reid arms (a stag's head, and over it a mitre, and the letters R.R.) Beside this there is a figure in a niche which is popularly supposed to represent Bishop Reid but Sir Henry Dryden argues that " the long hair and short tunic prevents its being Bishop Reid." The public, up till a few years ago, had free access to the tower, but, owing to the unsafe condition of the stairs, the door is now kept locked.

An Old Gold Seal.

We now turn once more into Broad Street, and going northward, past the front of the Cathedral, we come to the Strynd, on the east side of Broad Street. In this lane, between thirty and forty years ago, when some excavations were being made, a beautiful old gold seal was found among the rubbish, the accompanying being a correct wood-cut of the impression.

Wending our way eastwards along this lane, we get a good view of the Burgh School, which is seated to accommodate 500 scholars. Striking to the left into King Street, we pass the Free Church and Manse, and going through Queen Street, we turn down Catherine Place, which is on our left. We then strike to the right into Young Street, and coming up from the shore on our left hand will be seen a large block of old buildings which are known locally as " Dunkirk," but how the name originated is not known. A few minutes' walk now brings us to

Cromwell's Fort.

After the execution of Charles I., on the 30th of January, 1649, it was arranged by the Duke of Montrose to send an expedition from Orkney in favour of the Royal House. But disaster attended the movement from the very outset. At the beginning of 1650, twelve hundred troops were embarked at Gottenburg, but eleven of the ships got crushed in the ice, and only two reached Orkney, with about four hundred soldiers. These, with about two thousand untrained Orcadian soldiers, left Holm, Orkney, in April 1650 ; and on the 27th of the same month, they were attacked at Corbiesdale, near the Invercarron pass. The foreigners seem to have showed a little resistance, but the Orcadians at once threw down their arms and asked for quarter. A bloody slaughter ensued—over 200 being slain, 1,200 were taken prisoners, and the greater part of those who escaped from the battlefield were afterwards killed or captured by the Earl of Sutherland's followers. Cromwell's troops were quartered at Kirkwall during the Protectorate, when they erected this fort. The selection of The Mount, which commands the whole bay, showed that Cromwell's Ironsides knew their business well. The soldiers seem to have been pretty much given to pilfering. Among the enormities recorded against them is, that they broke open Bishop Tulloch's tomb, and stole bells from the Deerness Church. However, it is an "ill wind that blaws naebody guid." The Cromwellian soldiers are credited with having introduced an improved system of agriculture, and to have taught the use of the spinning-wheel, and the art of making locks and keys.

Having now had a peep at the various places of interest in the town, the tourist will better return to his hotel, and take the rest necessary to enable him to accompany us next day.

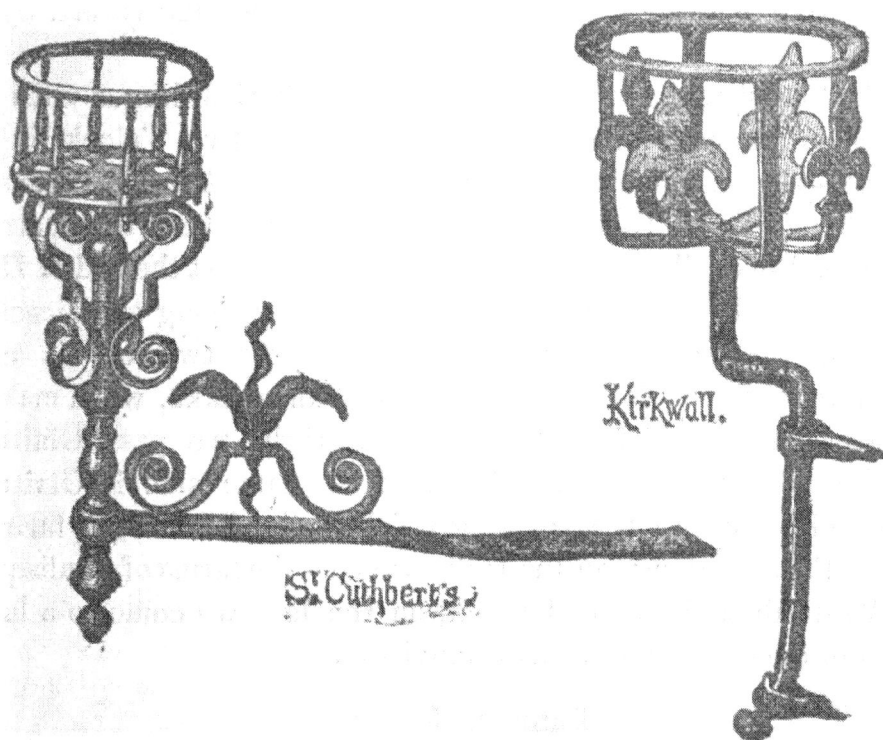

METAL STANDS FOR SAND-GLASSES USED IN ST MAGNUS CATHEDRAL, KIRKWALL, AND ST CUTHBERT'S, EDINBURGH.

WIDEFORD HILL.

THE distance from Kirkwall to the top of this hill is about **three** miles—the hill itself being about 730 feet high. Every May morning the youth and beauty of Kirkwall ascend it, at an early hour, for the purpose of bathing in "May dew." There are two roads leading to it—one along the Ayre, and up past Grainbank; the other by Walliwall, which runs from the south end of the town. For the sake of variety, we shall go by the latter, and return by the west.

If the tourist wishes to enjoy a sight which shall linger with him as long as memory lasts, he will start about two o'clock in the morning—the best months being June, July, or August. Passing along the streets of Kirkwall towards the south, he will be struck by the tomb-like silence which reigns supreme. At the end of High Street, we strike off into Walliwall road—this being the direction which Sir Walter Scott, in *The Pirate*, makes two of his chief characters (Captain Cleveland and John Bounce) take, when making an excursion to Wideford Hill. On the right we pass Glaitness School, a few yards further along, on the same side is Glaitness House, whilst up on the rising ground to the left is the farm of Corse. Further along, on the right, we pass the farms of Soulisquoy and Walliwall, and a little beyond, on the left, we come to a large stretch of moorland, known as Sunnybank.

Lammas Market.

This place is famous, from the fact that almost from time immemorial the Fair of St Ola, or, as it is now called, Lammas Market, has been held here. At one time the fair or market lasted fourteen days at least, and was patronised by the natives from all parts of the islands, whilst large numbers of travelling merchants from the south attended, and drove a roaring trade. In later years, however, the market has been shorn of much of its ancient glory, and only lasts two days at the beginning—Tuesday and Wednesday—and one day at the end—the last Saturday of the market.

Leaving the Market Stance, we push along a short distance, and then strike up the road to the right, near the farm of Sunnybank. At the end of this short road, we enter the wild heather, which is something like knee-deep. Here the ascent is sharp, though short, but there is little difficulty in scrambling to the hill top.

The View from the Top of Wideford Hill.

Lying at the foot of the hill, the town of Kirkwall presents a very pleasing picture. The ancient Cathedral of St Magnus, standing conspicuous in simple grandeur, with its dark red hues contrasting strongly with the white walls of the houses around, is no inapt memorial of the sanguinary period during which it was erected. In the immediate vicinity of the Cathedral are seen the stately ruins of the ancient palace of the Bishops of Orkney—a building of massive structure and warlike aspect—and the still more magnificent ruins of the princely palace erected by Patrick Stewart, Earl of Orkney, the whole forming a picturesque group which is probably unequalled by any other in Scotland. To the north of the town the scenery is grand. The dark gloomy like hills of North Ronaldshay in the far distance, and of Eday and Rousay in the nearer prospect, seem to add to the brightness of the verdure of the well cultivated fields of Sanday, Stronsay, Shapinsay, and Egilsey. To the south may be seen the dreaded Pentland Firth; and, if the morning is clear, the Sutherland Hills may be dimly descried in the distance, whilst the waters of Scapa Flow gently lave the shore lying at our feet. Westwards, the view is bounded by the Sandwick Hills. A glimpse will he had, nearer hand, of the far-famed Standing Stones of Stenness, whilst from where we stand the hills of Firth, Rendall and Evie stretch out in one vast chain of purple moorland, the gentle southern slopes of which are well cultivated, and in summer present a brilliant appearance. Turning our attention to the east, Copinshay and the Moul Head of Deerness are seen, whilst looking out in a straight line from Balfour Castle, if the morning be clear, Fair Isle will be seen like a spec on the horizon. But the grandest view of all, is the rising sun. Away over the wide expanse of water, streaks of purple and gold begin to diffuse the sky, darting like fiery tongues in all directions. These are followed by silvery gleams—now bright, then dim—as if trying the effect of light and shade. Something like a fiery vapour creeps up the sky, and the curtain is withdrawn—the sun red as a ball of fire, devours the last lingering shadows, and we have before us a picture of such dazzling brightness and splendour, as is fitted to fill the beholder with awe and admiration.

Pictshouses.

Proceeding down the western declivity of the hill, we come to a pictshouse, which was opened by the late Mr Petrie in 1849. It contains four apartments. The central one is ten feet long, five feet wide, and seven and a half feet high. The three other cells are respectively six and a half feet, six feet, and five and a half feet high ; and at the bottom from five and a half to six feet in length, and from three and a half to four and a half in width. The several passages forming the communications between the cells are about fifteen to eighteen inches high, and twenty-two inches wide. The entrance had been by a passage of similar dimensions, opening towards the west. From about a foot or two from the bottom of the cells each successive course of stones overlaps a little the one immediately beneath, by which means the walls gradually converge towards the top of the cell, which is not above a foot square (with the exception of the centre apartment). The latter was about two-thirds filled with earth and stones, appearing to have been poured down from an opening at the top. This heap was mixed with great quantities of the bones of the horse, cow, sheep, swine, dog, etc., the bones of the larger animals being nearest the bottom. A number of large ribs and other bones were lying in the mouths of the passages leading into the two cells branching off from each end of the central chamber.   Amongst them was a jaw bone, at first supposed to belong to a large deer. It was afterwards sent to Dr Daniel Wilson, of Edinburgh, by whom it was submitted to Mr Queeket, and Dr Falconer, of the Royal College of Surgeons in London, and was by them believed to belong to the *Bos Longifrons*, a district species of fossil ox.   In January 1854, it was exhibited along with four crania of the same species before the Royal Physical Society, Edinburgh, by Dr John Alexander Smith, who stated that this is the most ancient of the small sized cattle, being found in the drifts and fresh water deposits of the newer Pliocene formation, along with the remains of the huge animals of that time, the elephant and the rhinocerous, and downwards through the deposits of the alluvium to the times of man, shortly after which it becomes lost as a species, probably remaining in some of the domestic cattle as its later posterity.   Dr Smith considered the jaw bone found in the pictshouse on Wideford Hill especially worthy of notice, as proving the existence of this small ox in the Orkney Islands at a very early period, when the country in all probability was inhabited by some of the primitive races of our land, and he believed it was the first instance of its existence being noticed so far to the north in Britain. Dr Smith further stated that if we view the Orkney specimen as that of a domesticated ox, it is very interesting, as it may be considered an additional evidence of the inhabitants of this country having tamed an original native breed, it being by no means likely that in this comparatively remote place the domesticated ox could have been derived, as has been supposed, from the cattle introduced, it may be into the southern parts of Britain by the Roman colonists.   Mr Hugh Miller stated at the same meeting that he considered specimens of the kind exhibited by Dr Smith of much interest, also, in another point of view, as proving the direct descent of the animals of the present time from those of the latest geologic period ; showing that no era of convulsion had then taken place, but that races had since gradually become extinct by less direct and violent agency.

The Bos-Longifrons is generally understood to have become

wholly extinct in Britain as a distinct species about the time of the Roman invasion, though by some it is believed to have disappeared at a much earlier date. This apparently insignificant fragment of bone, therefore, goes far to prove that the Pictshouse on Wideford Hill was built not later than the 2d century of the Christian era, while at the same time judging from remains found in other buildings of its class it was in all probability erected many centuries earlier.

Leaving this we turn to the right, and proceed on our way back to Kirkwall· A short walk brings us to the farm of Quanterness, where there is a chambered mound which is fully described in Barry's History of Orkney. This mound is in the shape of a truncated cone, 14 ft. high, and 384 ft. in circumference. The passage is 1 ft. 9 in. broad and 2 ft. high. The large central apartment is 21 ft. 6 in. long, 6 ft. 6 in. broad, and 11 ft. 6 in. high. On the west side there are two small apartments, one being 10 ft. 7 in. long, 4 ft. 1 in. broad, and 7 ft. 6 in. high ; and the other 9 ft. 5 in. long, 4 ft. 5 in. broad, and 7 ft. high. On the east side there are other two small apartments—the dimensions of these being respectively 10 ft. long, 4 ft. 1 in. broad, and 8 ft. 6 in. high ; and the other 7 ft. 2 in. long, 3 ft. 9 in. broad, and 8 ft. 7 in. high.

We now leave Quanterness and travel along the public road leading to Kirkwall, till we reach the old farm house of Saverock, near the shore on our left. Here there is a Pictshouse, which has evidently been scooped out of the natural surface of the ground. Near the entrance there is a chamber in ruins. The passage is 47 ft. in length, and has been about 2 ft. 7 in. high, with an equal breadth. Nine feet below the surface is the principal chamber, which "forms an irregular pentagonal figure roughly stated to be 9 ft. in diameter. The height of the enclosing walls varies from 3 ft. to 4 ft. 6 in. The space within the chamber is very much reduced by the method taken to form the roof, which is by placing stone blocks or pillars, five in number, 2½ or 3 ft. high, and 1 ft. square, from 6 to 18 inches from the walls. Triangular flags are then laid with one angle resting on the pillars, other flags projected a little forwards rest upon these, and so on, till by continued over-lapping a rude conical-shaped roof is formed, which at the centre would be 5 or 6 ft. in height. A large lintel fire-place 5 ft. in length and 18 in. square, rests upon two pillars at the entrance of the chamber."

Ruined Circular Tower or Burg.

Returning to the public road, we make direct for Kirkwall, till we reach the farm of Grain, when we enter a field to the right, where there is a subterraneous chamber, which was explored in 1857. The walls were found to be in a ruinous condition. Amongst the *debris* was found pieces of deers' horns, quantities of ashes, portions of burnt bones and shells, and bits of charcoal, etc. The curved passage terminates in a built cell or chamber of an irregular oval shape about 13 feet long, and 6 feet of average width, and from 5 to 6 feet in height. There are two large blocks of stones placed upright, one on each side of the cell, about three feet from its entrance, and about a foot from the wall. Three feet further in, other two stones are similarly placed. They are all about a foot square, from $4\frac{1}{2}$ to 5 feet high. These blocks have stones projecting from the walls, and resting on them to support the roof of the cell. The roof is formed by large stones laid lengthways and across the cell. The passage is about 23 or 24 feet in length, from 2 feet 3 to 2 feet 8 inches in breadth, and about 3 feet high. It is evident, from the mass of ruins above and around the cell, that there has been a large building on the spot, and from a careful comparison of it with similar structures in Orkney in a less dilapidated state, there is good reason to believe that the cell was a place of concealment beneath one of the large circular towers or burgs, similar to those discovered at Burray and Birsay, and which are referred to elsewhere. There is evidence in the many ruins of round towers which still exist in Orkney, that the number of such buildings has at one time been very considerabl . They are from 50 to 60 feet in diameter from outside to outside of wall. The walls are from 12 to 15 feet thick, and, judging from the mass of ruins still remaining in some cases, must have originally been not less than 30 feet in height, and probably much more. They have, therefore, been very massive and imposing buildings, and display considerable ingenuity in the construction of the entrances, which were admirably adapted for defence.

A few minutes' walk now brings us back to Kirkwall, with, let us hope, a capital appetite, after our morning's exercise.

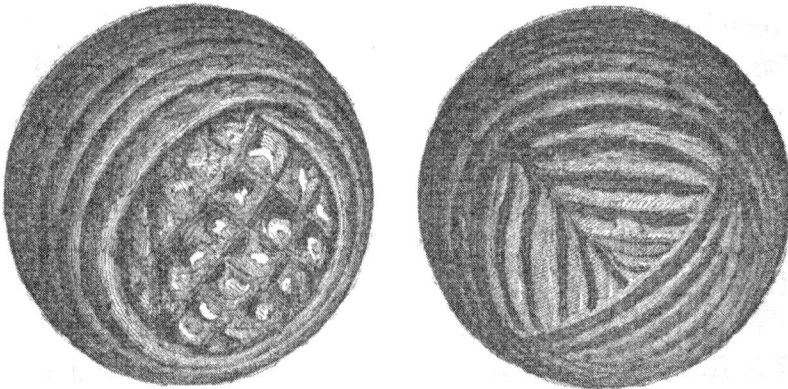

ORNAMENTED STONE BALL FOUND AT HILL HEAD, NEAR KIRKWALL.

A TRIP BY SEA AND LAND.

BY way of a little variation, we propose to have a short circular trip, going to the islands of Rousay, Egilsey, and Gairsay by sea, and then taking a run through some of the most attractive parishes in the west mainland, before returning to Kirkwall.

The little steamer Lizzie Burroughs leaves Kirkwall during the summer months on Tuesdays, Wednesdays, Thursdays, and Saturdays, for Rousay, &c. The sail to Rousay is generally short and pleasant—not occupying more than about three hours, which includes calls at intermediate ports. The steamer sails close to the land most of the way, so that a fine view of the scenery on both sides of the bay can be had. The first place of call is Rendall, after which Gairsay, Evie, and Egilsey are all touched at, the steamer dropping anchor at

Rousay.

This island lies near the northern extremity of the Mainland of Orkney. It abounds with objects of interest to the antiquarian, and is well worth the study of the archæologist on account of its ruins, pictshouses, standing stones, &c. Its physical aspects are variegated and highly picturesque, bearing a close resemblance in its scenery to the Western Highlands. There are two ranges of hills running from west to east, with lochs between, which give it a grand and picturesque appearance.

A public road runs right round the island, and is nearly 14 miles in length. Ascending the hill facing Trumbland Pier, a few minutes' walk brings us to Trumbland House, the mansion of Lieut.-General

Burroughs, the proprietor of nearly the whole island. Situated in the picturesque valley of Trumbland, the mansion has a very imposing appearance. The building is in the old Scottish baronial style of architecture. When erected, the house was surrounded by heather. But this bleak surrounding is being fast swept away—the purple heather giving place to green fields and waving grain. From this point we get a good view of the Established and U.P. Churches, which stand quite close together on the shore at Trumbland. Just above the Church, may be seen Cubberow's burden, which looks like a knowe with stones on the top of it. The tradition regarding this is that Cubberow was going to build a bridge across the Sound to Viera, but he had only got to this mound when the "fettle" of the keshie broke, and the giant was so disgusted he gave up the project.

Winding our way up the hill, half-an-hour's climbing brings us to the summit of Knitchinfield, which caps Blotchinfield, and which is 811 feet in height—being the highest hill in Rousay. From this point a grand view can be had of the whole Orkneys, whilst with the aid of a good glass, and if the day be fine, Foula in Shetland may be seen.

Going down the west slope of Blotchenfield Hill, we pass the Camp of Jupiter Fring, a romantic spot which tradition says was the haunt of eagles. To the south-west, the hill Marlariar attracts attention. Leaving the Camps, we come down the hill towards the Canny Stones, which are about twelve in number, and are near the Little Water. Above this will be seen a large stone, known as the Clet of Westness, upon which there are finger marks. Tradition has it that this stone was thrown by Cubberow from Westray to here. Little Water, and its companion, Muckle Water, are two fresh water lochs, in which good trout fishing may be had. Looking away to the east, the valley opens up—showing an unbroken picture of heather and water.

Taking a westerly direction, we come to the Mouthless Geo, which is a large gully, and shuts out from view everything except Burgar Roost, between Enhallow and Evie. We now approach the farm of Westness, the hills above which are beautifully terraced.

The gardens here are well worth seeing—being very prettily laid out. Situated W.S.W. we see the little island of Enhallow.

Striking now to the north, we come to Swein Bay, were there are the remains of an old pictshouse. Near this is Skail Church, which is in ruins, but, nevertheless, is quite a modern building. Passing along towards Brugh, we come to the remains of a pictshouse. Upon reaching Scabra Head, we see "Whale Roost," which runs at the rate of seven knots an hour. Near here is Paradise Geo, in which boatmen often take shelter whilst waiting for a favourable tide. It was at Scabra Head, Swein, the Viking, is said to have captured Jarl Paul—the latter being engaged in hunting otters at the time. The capture was not made, however, without much bloodshed, as is testified by the green mounds scattered around. Annexed is a stone sword, found near this place. Could it have been used by one of the friends of Paul or Swein in the bloody struggle?

A little beyond this we get a glimpse of a few magnificent arches, formed by Nature herself, in the most grotesque, yet attractive fashion, and known as Auk Hall, and Hole of the Horse. These places are the resorts of innumerable sea-birds—especially auks—which may be seen sitting, as the Rousay folk say, like bottles on the shelves of a whisky shop.

The large sea-caves, the Sinians of Cut-claws, are the next attraction. Twenty minutes' walk then brings us to the Kiln of Dusty, near Lobist—where the cliffs are high and bold—the highest, Hellia Spur, being about 400 feet to the top. The stack of Lobist is a massive pillar detached from the range of cliffs, by a chasm about seven yards wide, and bravely meets the incessant shocks of the Atlantic.

A little to the east of this is Whey Geo. Along this, under Sacquoy Head, are what are known as the "Covenanters' Caves," which, however, can only be seen from the sea. A little north of this are the Kilns of Brin Novir. Two of these gloups are easy of access, and through the natural arches formed by dame Nature, a fine view of the sea can be had. The other Kiln, however, is a very wild spot—over which the sea washes continually, and in all states of the tide.

On the east side of Sackquoy Head, near Saviskail, is a large geo which is known by the not very attractive name of Stinkina Geo—so-called, we believe, from the fact that large quantities of sea ware are washed into it, and rots—the consequence being that a bad odour hovers over it at certain periods of the year. At high tide boats have gone long distances into this geo, but how far it runs under the island has never yet been ascertained.

The rest of the rock scenery here is comparatively tame, so that it is best to cut straight across for Saviskail—where there is a nice little loch—Wasbister—which is about fifty acres in extent. Around this loch may be seen the remains of no less than four old chapels. Near the graveyard is Corse Kirk ; at Bretaness is another ; close to the sea at Langskail is a third, dedicated to St Colm ; whilst on the holm in the loch is the chapel of Burrian.

From Saviskail we strike off in an easterly direction for Lyan, where the rocks are very precipitous. Cubberow is also said to have pitched a stone from Westray to Lyan, and his finger marks may be seen on it! We now ascend Kierfa Hill, which is 762 feet high, and from which we get a magnificent view of all the islands in Orkney, as well as Foula, in Shetland, and the Western Highlands. We now strike out for the Head of Faraclet. Here there is a splendid cave, which may be explored by those who have sufficient nerve to descend by means of a rope. From the knee of Faraclet a good view is to be had of Westray, Eday, Stronsay, and Shapinsay, &c. On the S.W. of Faraclet near Scockness, will be seen the remains of some pictshouses.

Leaving this, we pass through Sourin, when a smart walk of about an hour brings us back to our starting point at Trumbland.

Having now explored Rousay, we shall hurry round to Westness, where for a trifle we will get a boat to take us across a narrow stretch of sea, which separates Enhallow from Rousay—a distance of three quarters of a mile or so.

Enhallow.

This small island (the holy island) is the property of Col. Balfour, of Balfour and Trenabie. It is marked by tradition as a spot on which neither mice, rats, or cats, can live. On the S.W. slope of the island there are the remains of an old chapel, which for a long time was used as a dwelling house, and when the old buildings were being demolished, the chapel was discovered. Sir Henry Dryden, who examined the building very minutely, conjectures that the first portion of it was built in the 11th or 12th century, whilst in the 14th century a few additions were made to it.* At the face of the cliffs is a cave known as Nine Men's Hole, where nine Rousay men are said to have hid to escape the Press Gang.

Returning to the little boat, a short sail down Enhallow Sound, brings us to

Viera, or Wyre.

This small island is the property of Lieutenant-General Burroughs, and, according to the *Orkneyinga Saga*, was the place of residence of that " very over-bearing man," Kolbein Hruga, who collected the King of Norway's taxes in Orkney. Kolbein Hruga, seems to have lived like a little monarch. He built for himself a castle, known as " Cubberow " Castle, from which he could effectively defend himself from the onslaughts of his enemies. Near this ruined castle are the remains of an old chapel, which Sir Henry Dryden thinks must have been built in the 12th or 13th centuries. †

Our little boat will now carry us across Rousay Sound, and we land at

Egilsey,

Which is the property of Dr Baikie of Tankerness, and has been owned by that family now for over 600 years. To the antiquarian, this island is one of the most interesting in the group. The Orkney

---

* For full description of Chapel see Appendix A.
† For full description of Wyre Chapel, see Appendix A.

islands were early visited by the missionaries of St Columba, and not long after their entire subjugation by the Picts they were visited by St Serf. The erection of churches, and the settlement of Papæ or priests in various localities, resulted from the labours of these Culdee missionaries. And it is interesting to know that the church of Egilsey, with its curious round tower, was erected by them, as its peculiar style of architecture corresponds with the primitive churches of the sixth and seventh centuries. Professor Munch of Christiania, in a letter on the island, says he "Now feels quite sure that the name of Egilsey is not, as it would seem to be at the first glance, a composition of the *nom. proprium* ' Egill ' (a man's name) and ' ey ' (island) ; but to be derived from the Gaelic corruption ' eglais' or 'eglis' of the Latin ' *ecclesia*,' and probably signifying 'Church-Island,' because of the venerable church still existing, and undoubtedly belonging to the ante-Norwegien era, viz., to the Irish Culdees or ' Papæ' standing there already at the arrival of the first Vikings about A.D. 800. The name, however, has been twisted into a more Norwegian-looking form, and perhaps, in later times, believed by the ignorant population really to derive its origin from some ancient Viking called ' Egill.'" No ordinary degree of interest thus attaches to this ancient edifice, which, for upwards of a thousand years, has been so intimately associated with many of the stirring and too often tragic events that have occurred in Orkney.

The Cathedral, which is known by the name of St Magnus, is a conspicuous object from all sides, and is seen from great distances. It is on the west side of the island. The date of its erection is unknown ; but is supposed to have been long prior to mediæval times. It is the oldest building now extant in Orkney. It derived its name from the tradition that Magnus, one of the Earls of Orkney, was murdered in or near the place where it stands, about 1110. Till within the last sixty years it was used as a place of worship—the late Mr Paterson of Rousay having preached in it every alternate Sabbath. Its architecture is very peculiar—many of the thin flat stones being built into the walls on their edges. The form of the arches, both of doors and windows, is said to be a combination of

Grecian and Roman, but imperfectly executed. The portion which served for a chancel is arched over in the interior. In later times, it is said the "Cutty Stool" was placed here, and from the fact of there being no window to afford light, it must have been a suitable position for this once famous piece of ecclesiastical furniture. On the west end is a tower, circular in form, built into gables of rough stone, rising to a height of about 40 feet, with a slight lean westward.*

With a favourable breeze, a short sail will transfer us to the island of

Gairsay,

The property of Col. Balfour of Balfour and Trenabie. On the south shore of the island are to be seen the ruins of the mansion house of the Craigies, supposed to have been built at the end of the 17th century. At that period the Craigies were a distinguished family, and the loop holes in the building show that they were in a position to defend themselves from intruders. Just outside the mansion, there are the ruins of an old chapel. Gairsay was the headquarters of Swein Asleifson, the Viking, whose many feats of daring are chronicled in the *Orkneyinga Saga.*

"Swein used to reside at home in Gáreksey, in winter, keeping there eighty men at his own expense. He had such a large drinking-hall that there was none equal to it anywhere else in the Orkneys. In the spring he was very busy sowing a large breadth of seed, and he usually did a great part of the work himself. When this work was finished, he went every spring on marauding expeditions. He plundered in the Sudreyar and Ireland, and returned home after midsummer. This he called spring-viking. Then he stayed at home till the fields were reaped and the corn brought in. Then he went out again, and did not return until one month of winter had passed. This he called autumn-viking."

When Swein went on his last marauding excursion, he took with him seven large long-ships. On reaching Dublin, the *Orkneyinga Saga* says Swein and his men surprised the people, "took a great deal of

* A full description of the Church is given in Appendix A.

plunder, and took captive the rulers of the city, and their negotia-
tions ended in the surrender of the town to Swein, and they promised
to pay as much money as he might levy on them. He was to
quarter his men on the town, and have the command of it, and the
Dýflin men confirmed this arrangement with oaths. Swein and his
men went down to their ships in the evening, but in the morning
they were to come into the town and receive hostages from the
inhabitants. Now it is to be told what was going on in the town
during the night. The rulers of the town had a meeting, and
considered the difficulties in which they were placed. They thought
it a grievous hardship that they should have to surrender their town
to the Orkneymen, especially to him whom they knew to be the
most exacting man in the whole west; and they came to the
determination to play him false if they could. They resolved to
dig large pits inside of the city gates, and in many other places
between the houses, where it was intended that Swein's men should
come in, and armed men were hidden in the houses close by. They
placed such coverings over the pits as were sure to fall in when the
weight of the men came upon them. Then they covered all over
with straw, so that the pits could not be seen, and waited till
morning. Next morning Swein and his men arose and armed themselves, and went to the town; and when they came near the gates
the Dýflin (Dublin) men ranged themselves on both sides from the
gates along by the pits. Swein and his men, not being on their
guard, fell into them. Some of the townsmen ran immediately to
the gates, and others to the pits, and attacked Swein's men with
weapons. It was difficult for them to defend themselves, and Swein
perished there in the pit, with all those who had entered the town.
It was said that Swein was the last man who died there, and that he
spake these words before his fall: 'Know all men, whether I die
to-day or not, that I am the holy Earl Rögnvald's henchman, and my
confidence is where he is with God.' Swein's surviving followers
went then to their ships, and put out to sea; and nothing is said of
their voyage until they came to the Orkneys. Here is the end of
Swein's history; and it has been said that he was the greatest man

in the Western lands, either in olden times or at the present day, of those who had not a higher title than he had."

We now cross the water to the Mainland again—landing at Tingwall,

Rendall.

At this point we should have a machine awaiting our arrival. Taking our seats in it, we drive through the well cultivated parish of Rendall. A run of three miles brings us to

Evie.

When we reach Burgar, we can leave our conveyance for a few minutes, and pay a visit to the round tower here. These towers are circular in form, and in some cases have two concentric walls, with chambers between. In other cases the wall is 14 or 15 feet across, and contains cells within it. The area enclosed by the circular wall is generally from 30 to 40 feet. This tower of Burgar is of this class, with the concentric walls. In it has been found a human skeleton, with a rude bone comb, and a piece of deer's horn lying beside it, in one of the chambers. Although it is doubtful whether the body was placed there while the Brugh was inhabited, or after it became a ruin, still the discovery of the comb and deer's horn, especially the latter, shows that the building belongs to a very early period.

Resuming our journey, we have a beautiful drive along the west shore,—the scenery of land and sea being very effective. Near Costa Head, the road branches off to the left, and we enter

Birsay,

At Swannay, and a drive of about two miles now brings us to the Barony, where we will leave our machine, and pay a visit to the Earl's Palace, which lies close to the shore. Lord Robert Stewart forced the people to build this mansion for him. He placed over the gateway a stone with the following inscription:—" Dominus Robartus Stewartus Filius Jacobi Quinti *Rex* Scotorum hoc opus instruxit." When Patrick, Earl Robert's son, was tried for treason, this inscription was used in evidence against him—the construction put upon it being that Earl Robert had assumed the title of King of Scotland.

"The palace originally consisted of a range of buildings forming four sides of a court which measured 104 ft. 3 in., N. and S., by 59 ft. 9 in. E. and W. The external measurements are 172 ft. 2 in. N. and S., by 120 ft. 10 in. E. and W. At the S.E., N.E., and S.W. angles are square projecting towers, and the main entrance was in the south wall. At the N. is a portion of an older building. A modern wall has been built connecting the two flanking towers at the S. end, inside of which can still be seen the traces of the old wall. The whole building is now the remains of a shell, and the best portion is the older part, which has been attributed to the St Clairs."*

Supposing we are fortunate enough to be here at ebb tide, we will get across to the Brough, on which is the remains of St Peter's Chapel, which Sir Henry Dryden thinks was built about 1100, by Erlend, the father of St Magnus.†

Retracing our steps to the Mainland, we proceed southwards from the palace, amongst the sandy knowes, and after ascending towards Marwick for a short distance, we reach the Knowe of Saverough, which was opened by Mr Farrer, M.P., in 1862, who communicated the result of his investigations to the *Orcadian* newspaper of August 9, 1862. Mr Farrer said :—

"The Knowe is on the property of the Earl of Zetland, and is close to the sea. It is almost entirely composed of sand, either deposited in ancient times or drifted by the wind. The skeletons, of which the subjoined account is given, lay at depths varying from two to eight or ten feet, and were in different stages of preservation. Those which were nearest to the surface were most decayed. Not a vestige of any article of dress was discovered. The sand was only slightly discoloured. Fibrous roots of grasses had grown through and around some of the skeletons, and from the mass of sand above them, and in which no symptoms of vegetation appeared, it seems probable

* The Orkneys and Shetland.
† For full description see Appendix A.

that much of the sand had been blown over the graves since their interment. The Knowe is rather flat at the top, with a slight depression towards the centre. The heads of the skeletons all faced the north-west, with the exception of two, which were towards the north. The kists in which they were entombed were generally broken by the weight of the superincumbent sand. The bodies had flagstones under them in only a few instances. The teeth were sound, but worn quite smooth. None of them presented the usual appearance of the canine or dog-teeth. Some of the skulls were in an extraordinary state of preservation. I have sent them all (with the exception of No. 2) to Dr Thurnam of Devizes for examination. Some appeared to be of a very low type, perhaps the Kumbe-Kephalic or boat shaped form, as described by Professor Wilson in his Pre-historic Annals of Scotland—and others—and those the best preserved, of a much higher class.

" No. 1.—The head slightly inclined, and the mouth open ; the body laid flat, the ribs in their natural position, and the arms by the side of the body ; the left hand was rested on a small flat stone, the vertibræ of the back were forced up between the ribs, roots of grasses and sand filled up the interstices.

" No. 2.—At the head of this skeleton, on the right side, was an urn of baked clay, filled with sand, 5 inches high, $5\frac{1}{2}$ in. diameter at the top, and $3\frac{1}{2}$ at the base. The skeleton lay on its back. There was a small circular hole at the back of the head as if it had been perforated by an arrow—possibly the death-wound. The upper part of the body lay as originally deposited, but the lower extremities could not be distinctly traced. The leg bones and some of the toe joints were found, but separated from the body. Possibly, however this was caused by the workmen in cleaning away the sand. The skull of this skeleton, together with the urn, has been forwarded to the Museum of Scottish Antiquaries, Edinburgh.

" No. 3.—This skull was deposited above No. 2. No teeth were found. It was less well preserved than No. 2, and the form of the skeleton could not be made out. The skull appeared to be of the lower class.

" No. 4 was similar in character. It lay above, and not far from No. 1.

" No. 5.—Only fragments of skull and bones.

" No. 6.—The legs of this skeleton were uppermost, and within two feet of the surface ; they were doubled back upon the ribs ; a large stone lay on the skeleton, the skull of which was broken in removing. It lay at no great distance from No. 2. The kist stones were displaced ; the head lay on its side. The body appeared to have been hurriedly interred.

" Nos. 7 and 7 A (so numbered because discovered after 8 and 9 had been disinterred) were very near the surface ; probably, however, the sand may have been blown away at no distant date. They were both much decayed, and the bones intermixed, and these also might have been interred in haste.

" No. 8.—This skull lay facing the north. The skeleton was laid flat, and was the most perfect of any that were found. The feet only were missing ; the teeth, as in the other skulls, were worn smooth. None of them were missing.

" No 9.—Only fragments of jaw, a little above No. 7. It is possible that these fragments may have belonged to that skeleton.

" No. 10.—Skull and bones ; head towards the North ; the end of the cover stone of the kist rested on the skull.

" No. 11.—The head of this skeleton was missing, nor could any portion of the skeleton below the knees be found.

" It is probable that many more skeletons are interred within the knowe, since only a small portion of it has been as yet explored. I do not venture to suggest at what period they were buried. The urn seems to indicate the lapse of many centuries, but some of the other bodies may have been interred more recently."

Proceeding eastwards, we come to the Okostro Brugh, which is very interesting from the proofs it has given of the antiquity of these buildings. In it a great number of kists or graves, 2 or 3 feet long, were first discovered. They contained burnt bones and ashes, and one of them was a large bowl shaped stone urn. The ruins of the Brugh were discovered beneath the kists, with some earth intervening. In cleaning out the area within the circular wall, a rude bone comb, and other bone implements, were picked up, also a curious stone lamp with a perforated handle, pieces of deer's horns, and other primitive relics.

It is evident that the Brugh must have been in ruins so long before the graves were made above it that a very considerable depth of earth had succumbed. And as the graves themselves prove by their contents that they belong to a period prior at all events to the introduction of Christianity among the Norwegians, and possibly also to its introduction among the earlier race of Celts in the 6th century, the Brugh must belong to a very early period. The relics found in it also go to prove this.

Returning to the Barony, we may now visit the Parish Church, which is said to occupy the site of Christ's Kirk. Built into the wall of the Church, there is a stone, which has inscribed upon it the word " Bellus." Antiquarians long discussed the meaning of the word, but nothing of any value came out of all that was written upon it.

Christ's Kirk was built about the middle of the 11th century by Thorfinn. He was one of the Jarls of Orkney, who was continually engaged in military enterprise, and of whom Arnór Jarlaskáld sings in the Saga—

> " Unto Thorfinn, ravens' feeder,
> Armies had to yield obedience
> From Thussasker right on to Dublin.
> Truth I tell, as is recorded.

Towards the close of his life Thorfinn visited Rome, after which he built this church, which he dedicated to Christ. According to the Saga, he was Earl for " seventy winters," and " his widow Ingibiorg was married to King Malcolm Canmore."

This Kirk is also famous because the remains of St Magnus were deposited here, and the Saga referring to this event says :—" Soon after this a heavenly light was seen above his burial place. Then men who were placed in danger began to pray to him, and their prayers were heard. A heavenly odour was frequently perceived above his burial-place, from which people suffering from illness received health, Then sufferers made pilgrimages thither both from the Orkneys and Hjaltland, and kept vigils at his grave, and were cured of all their sufferings.   But people dared not make this known while Earl Hákon was alive.   It is said of the men who were most guilty in the murder of the holy Earl Magnus that most of them met with a miserable death."

Should the tourist desire to spend a few hours here, there are three lochs in the vicinity where trouts are numerous, and of fair size —we refer to the Loch of Birsay and the Loch of Twatt.

Taking our seats in the conveyance once more, we resume our journey, and have a pleasant drive into Sandwick, a distance of about eight miles.   On a part of the road we have the loch of Harray on our left, across which we can see a large stretch of the parish of

Harray.

This parish is famous for two things—it is the only parish in Orkney which is untouched by the sea, and it can boast of about one hundred proprietors.   In 1860, when the new road was being made, a circular tower or burg was discovered. The diameter of the building was about 50 feet, and the thickness of the wall was from 12 to 15 feet.   In this parish old customs lingered long, and are only now wearing out.

Sandwick.

Leaving our conveyance at Skail, we take a walk along the coast, where the scenery is wild and grand.   Here will be seen the Castle of Yesnaby, a large pillar which is detached from the face of the cliffs, and stands there like a mighty sentinel, the wonder of all who have seen it.   On the summit of the precipices will be seen the figured stones of Skail, which were supposed by early writers to have been an artificial street.   Near here is the "Hole of Row," a very pretty natural arch.

Passing round to the south-eastern corner of the Bay of Skail we come to the Weens of Skara Brae, which contributed a most important addition to our knowledge of the pre-historic people of Orkney.   This structure is not subterranean like so many of the pictshouses, but has been built on the original surface]   It consists

of a long winding passage, which has been roofed over by large
flagstones, at a height of about 3 feet, so that it could only be entered
in a stooping position, and into which opened several chambers, which
have apparently been separate huts. They are nearly square—about
20 feet each way, with upright walls about 7 feet high and one foot
thick, but with the angles rounded off, and the walls, which are perpendicular at the sides, converging inwards at the angles. Several
cells and recesses are built into the walls, or project from them,
which may have been closets, or in some instances sleeping places,
and each chamber has had a fire in the centre, defined by a square
space paved with large hearth stones, and inclosed by low upright
flags. There was some appearance of the chambers having been
partially roofed by jaw bones of whales, some fragments of large
jaw bones having been found on the floor. On the whole, the appearance of the chamber was not unlike that of the interior fittings and
arrangements of the Burgs, when the later or secondary additions
common in the latter have been removed. The number of implements of stone and bone found in cleaning out the building, was quite
extraordinary. Several hundred objects were found, which showed
unequivocal proofs of having been wrought or selected by human
agency.

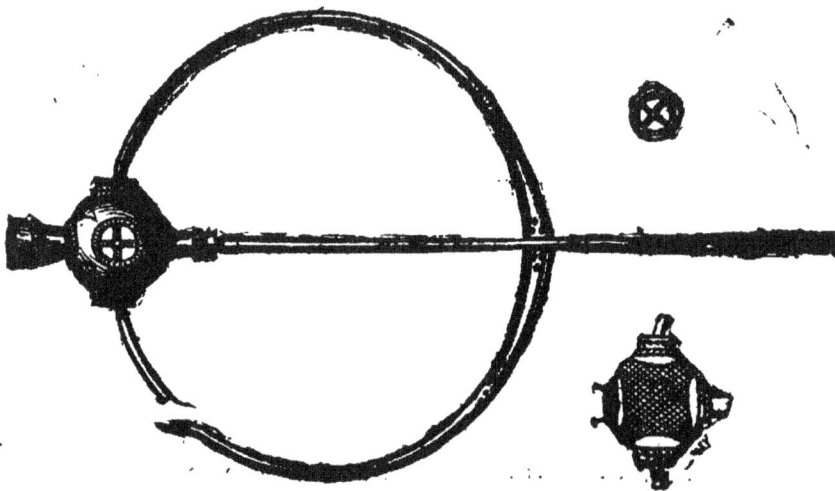

FANCY PIN FOUND AT SKAIL, SANDWICK.

About the beginning of 1858, a large number of silver articles were found on the shore of this bay, near the Parish Church. These consisted of large fibulaè, torcs or collars of chain of twisted rope patterns, armlets or bracelets, and a few coins. The coins were very perfect, and belonged to the tenth century; one of them being of the reign of the Anglo-Saxon King Athelstan or " Edelstan," about the middle of the tenth century.

ARMLET FOUND AT SKAIL.

Betaking ourselves once more to our conveyance, we have a drive of six miles or so, when we reach the Kirkwall and Stromness Road. Though we are now within easy distance of the latter place, we prefer meantime to strike to the left, till we reach the township of

Ireland, when we have a lovely drive of about six miles to our next halting place.

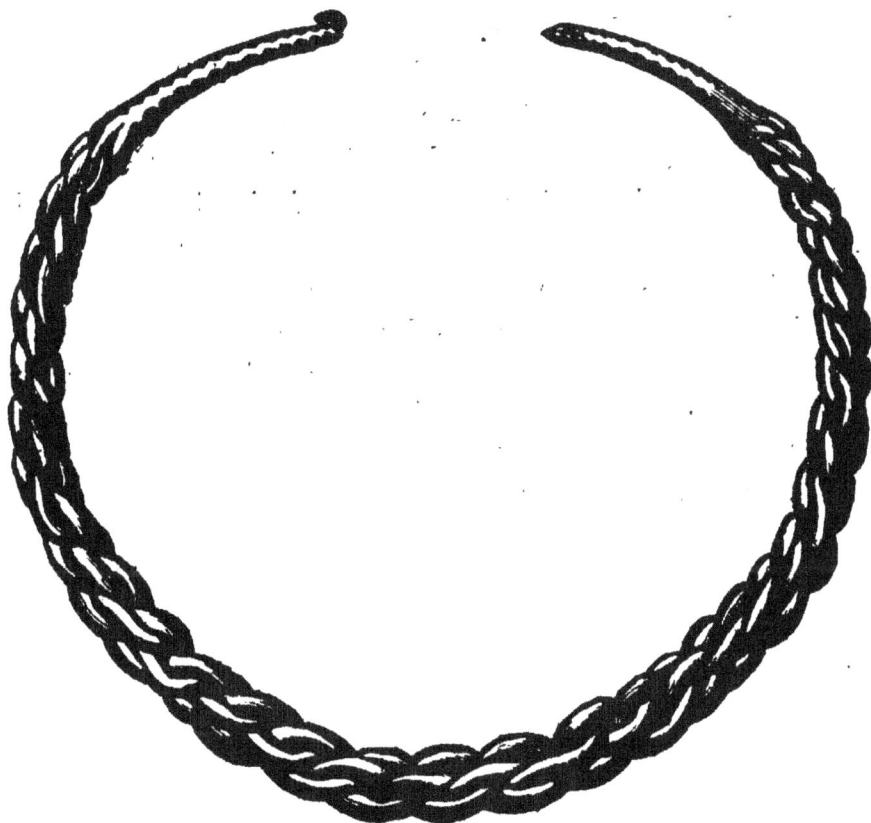

TORC OR COLLAR FOUND AT SKAIL.

Orphir.

From the hall of Clestrain, which is the first house in the Orphir parish, from this side, we have a drive of about three miles to the Free Church, where we strike off towards Houton Head, and the Established Church, which are down close to the sea shore. Leaving our machine here, we enter the graveyard, where stands a very remarkable ruin—the remains of a round church with semi-circular apse—which is immediately opposite to, and within a few feet of, the door of the present parish church.

A gentleman who had seen the present church in the course of erection, in 1829, stated that the remains of the wall attached to the apse were circular, and extended beneath the foundations of the parish church; and even now they can be traced up to its side walls, beneath which they disappear.

In the old Statistical Account of the parish of Orphir, there is the following account of the ruins :—" In the churchyard are the remains of an ancient building, called the Girth House, to which great antiquity is ascribed. It is a rotundo 18 ft. in diameter, and 20 ft. high, open at top, and on the east side is a vaulted concavity, where probably the altar stood, with a slit in the wall to admit the light; two-thirds of it have been taken down to repair the parish church. The walls are thick, and consist of stones strongly cemented with lime."

The measurements taken so far verify those given in the old Statistical Account, for the diameter is about 18 ft. 10 in. The walls have certainly been built with very strong mortar. The remains of the circular wall of the church are 3 ft. 10 in. thick. They extend only to about 8 ft. on each side of the apse ; and there is no appearance of door or window. The wall of the apse is two ft. 9 in. thick. The internal measurement of the apse is as follows :—width in front, 7 ft. 1 in.; height, 7½ ft.; depth, backwards to the window, 7 ft. 1 in. The sole of the window is 1 ft. 6 in. above the present level of the ground inside the apse. The opening of the window is 3 ft. high and 1 ft. wide. The frame for the glass has been 1 ft. from the outside, and the splay of the window gives a width of 1 ft. 6½ in. on the outside, and 1 ft. 7½ in. on the inside. The height of the window, including the splay, is, on the inside, 3 ft. 7 in., and on the outside 3 ft. 6 in. The distance from the ground to the spring of the arch of the apse is 4 ft. 6 in. on one side, and 4 ft. 3 in. on the other. The window is a few inches towards the north side from the centre of the wall of the apse, and looks eastward. The whole height of the apse, measuring from the level of the ground on the inside to the top of the ruin outside, is about 11 ft. The church has, evidently, from the name which it still bears, been the " Gyrth," or sanctuary for the district in former days.*

* For full particulars see Appendix A.

In the immediate neighbourhood of the graveyard are numerous traces of ancient buildings, which are believed to be the remains of the palace of Jarl Paul, who lived at Orphir in the twelfth century. During some excavations which were made about 1859, close to the outside of the churchyard wall, great quantities of bones of various domestic animals were found, and amongst them were jaw bones of dogs and cats in great abundance.

This old palace must have been a grand building—contained a *skali*, or banqueting hall—and was the scene of many strange and exciting incidents.

Two brothers, Earl Paul and Earl Harald, at one time reigned together in Orkney, but were always quarrelling. At last their friends got them to come to an understanding, and they agreed to spend Christmas and all the chief festivals together. One Christmas evening, Earl Harald had all his friends gathered around him at the palace here, and great preparations were made for having a big carousal. The sisters of the Earls—Frákork and Helga—were also there.

" Earl Harald went into the room where the sisters were sitting on a cross-bench, and saw a linen garment, newly made, and white as snow, lying between them. The Earl took it up, and saw that it was embroidered with gold. He asked, 'To whom does this splendid thing belong?'

" Frákork replied, 'It is intended for your brother Paul.'

" 'Why do you make such a fine garment for him? You do not take such pains in making my clothing.'

" He had just come out of bed, and was dressed in a shirt and linen drawers, and had thrown a mantle over his shoulders. He threw off the mantle, and spread out the dress. His mother took hold of it, and asked him not to envy his brother of his fine clothing. The Earl pulled it from her, and prepared to put it on. Then Frákork snatched off her head-gear, and tore her hair, and said that his life was at stake if he put it on, and both of the women wept grievously. The Earl put on the garment nevertheless; but as soon as it touched his sides a shiver went through his body, which was soon followed by great pain, so that he had to take to his bed; and he was not long in bed until he died.

"Earl Paul considered that the splendid underclothing which Earl Harald had put on had been intended for him, and therefore he did not like the sisters to stay in the Orkneys. So they left the Islands with all their attendants, and went first to Caithness, and then to Scotland, to the estate which Frákork had there."

A few years afterwards Earl Paul gave a grand feast in the Palace at Orphir. But the shadow of death hung over it. Valthiof, Olaf's son, with nine or ten men from Stroma, in going to the feast, were lost in the Pentland Firth. Yet the Palace party was merry. They seemed to pray and spree alternately.

After even song, they left the church, and entered the drinking hall, where there was a great feast, the effects of which had to be slept off. The company then rose to mass about midnight, after which they again entered the hall. The large room was brilliantly lighted by candle-boys, who held aloft lights, whilst others served out the drinking cups. Nones service followed, after which the guests drank to the memory of the departed heroes, out of large horns. Whilst this was going on, Swein Brióstreip began to quarrel with his namesake, Swein Asleifson, and was heard to mumble " Swein will be the death of Swein, and Swein shall be the death of Swein." This was taken to mean a threat of murder, so Swein Asleifson resolved to strike the first blow, and hid in the shadow in the passage till Swein Brióstreip and his friend Jón were leaving the drinking hall.

" When Swein Brióstreip came into the doorway, Swein Asleifson struck him on the forehead, so that he stumbled, but did not fall ; and when he regained his footing, he saw a man in the door, and thought it was he who had wounded him. Then he drew his sword, and struck at his head, splitting it down to the shoulders. This, however, was Jón, his kinsman, and they fell there both."

Leaving here, a drive of about three miles brings us to the Mill of Kirbuster, where we will make another short stay. At the Loch of Kirbuster, there is good trout fishing to be had. Above the north-west corner of the loch may be seen, at Oback, the ruins which are pointed out as being on the spot where the Earl of Caithness was slain after the battle of Summerdale. Near this the three hills—Acla, Wardhill, and Midhill—stand like a half-crescent, and a fine view can be had from each of them. The town of Stromness, romantically situated on the slope of Brinkie's Brae, the lochs of Swannay and Kierfiold to the north-west, and most of the islands, with the bays between, can all be seen to great advantage. Looking through Hoxa Sound we see the fine beach at Gillsbay, as well as some of the hills in Sutherlandshire. Here, too, we look down upon the battlefield of Summerdale, which was fought on the north side of this hill, and to which we have already alluded. In the year 1526, the Orcadians took the Castle of Kirkwall from Lord William Sinclair. In the following year he returned, accompanied with John, Earl of Caithness, and a large force. Upon landing, they determined to kill the first Orcadian they met. "This was in consequence of a witch, who had met them on landing, walking before them unwinding two balls of thread, one of blue and the other of red, and the thread of the latter having first become exhausted, she told the Earl of Caithness, that the side on which the first blood was shed would be defeated. Seeing a short time afterwards a boy herding cattle, the Earl at once slew him, and had hardly done so, when to his horror, the victim was recognised as a native of Caithness. This is supposed to have depressed the Caithness men before the fight. Nevertheless, they are said to have fought stoutly, till they were assailed by the Orcadians with stones, which were supposed to have been supplied by some miraculous interposition, as the ground, whereon the battle was fought, was on the previous day said to have been singularly free from stones. When these missiles commenced to fly about, a sudden panic seized the Caithness men, who, throwing their arms into the Loch of *Lummagem*, fled, and, the Orcadians having destroyed their boats, were slaughtered in detail. Barry states, that dead bodies had been found at the end of the last century in a marsh, through which the vanquished had fled, with the clothes still entire, owing to the antiseptic nature of the soil. . . . . .

The Orcadians are stated to have lost only one man, who, having attired himself in the clothes of one of the slaughtered Caithness men, was returning home at night, and was slain by mistake by his own mother with a stone in the foot of one of his own stockings."

We now resume our journey, and a drive of six miles brings us back to Kirkwall.

A TRIP to the EAST MAINLAND, BURRAY, and SOUTH RONALDSHAY.

THE drive from Kirkwall to Deerness is a very enjoyable one. As we ascend the hill at the first mile-stone on the Deerness road, we get a lovely view of Kirkwall, the bay, and the North Isles; whilst the String, bounded on one side by the island of Shapinsay, and on the other by the Mainland, looks like some fairy picture. As we descend the hill on the other side, we pass the burn of Wideford, the shrubbery here giving the landscape a romantic appearance. A drive of a few minutes brings us to the road which branches off towards

Tankerness,

Where is situated the mansion house of the Baikies. Around it a plantation is beautifully laid out, and thrives well. There is also a nice loch here. In connection with the estate there is a substantial pier, at which there is a fishing station.

We prefer, however, to strike direct for St Andrews and Deerness, and turn to the right, up the hill at New England. Here we pass through a long stretch of bleak moorland, a favourite resort of plover, snipe, and grouse. When we reach the summit of the hill we get glimpses of the Moul Head of Deerness, Copinsay, and the Pentland Skerries. Passing through the parish of

St Andrews,

The visitor will be struck with the large number of well cultivated farms which dot the country on each side of the public road. Here, too, as we pass through Toab, will be seen many grassy knolls, which are believed to be graves of the ancient inhabitants. In the parish there is the remains of a burg, but most of it has been used for building purposes. On the top of one of the knolls already referred to, it is said there was once a chapel ; on another, tradition says there was a Popish chapel ; and the rectangular space here is surrounded by a large number of stones, which are erected edgeways. At the point of Ness, one of Cromwell's forts may still be seen. As we approach

Deerness,

And descend the hill at the Sands of Dinghieshowe, the attention is at once attracted by the green knoll here, under which is the remains of the Burg of Dinghieshowe. From the top of the hill on the other side of the Ayre, a fine view of the Hoy Hills is got away in the west, whilst in the east, quite close to us, is Copinsay, and an adjoin- ing rock, known as the Horse of Copinsay. Between us and Copinsay is Corn Holm, where Low "found the remains of a small chapel 17 ft. by 15 ft., with walls 5 ft. thick, but low, and the door- way so low as to compel him to stoop on entering. Close to the chapel was a well with stairs leading down to it, and all around seem to have been scattered the remains of small buildings." If the trip to Deerness be made in May, we recommend a visit to Copinsay, where the sea-fowl are innumerable. In the early summer the Deerness people often go across and amuse themselves by descending the cliffs for auk eggs—a most exciting, and, we may add, rather a dangerous pursuit.

Passing Smiddybanks, a run of about two miles brings us to the Established Church, which has been built on the site of an old church, seen and described by Low as follows :—

" The Church of Deerness, is very remarkable, and part of it looks to be pretty ancient : the east end consists of a vault which crosses the breadth of the inside, and at each side of this is erected a small steeple. Thro' the vault or quire one enters the steeple on his right hand, and by a turnpike stair goes to a small apartment or vestry built between the steeples. From this last apartment he enters the second, which, or both probably, have had bells ; these are now gone, said to have been carried away by Cromwell's soldiers. Tradition is not clear (and there are no records) who was the builder of this Church. The steeples are said to be monumental, and placed over a Lady's two sons buried there, but whether this is so or not is hard to determine."

Tradition has it that persons married in this church were never very successful in life, and that young people therefore often went to St. Andrews to get united in matrimony.

Here the public road ends, so that we leave our conveyance, and make the rest of the journey on foot. Ten minutes' walk brings us to Sandside, where may be seen the ruins of the old mansion house of the Buchanans, who, two centuries ago, were amongst the great aristocrats of the islands. Low tells us that the chimney piece of one of their rooms was embellished with the following quaint question :—" Who can dwell with everlasting burnings ?"

It is supposed that the great sea-fight between Earl Thorfinn and Karl Hundason, was fought in the bay opposite this point. King Karl wanted Thorfinn to pay tribute for Caithness. This the latter would not do ; but plundered far and wide in Scotland. Karl got exasperated at this, and sailed to Orkney to take summary vengeance upon Thorfinn. When Karl's war-ships came in sight " there were only two alternatives—one to run on shore, and leave the ships with all their valuable contents to the enemy ; the other was to meet the King, and let fate decide between them. Earl Thorfinn exhorted his men, and ordered them to have their arms ready. He said he would not flee, and told them to row briskly towards the enemy. Then both parties fastened their ships together. Earl Thorfinn addressed his men, advising them to be smart and to make the first attack fiercely, and saying that few of the Scotsmen would be able to make a stand. The fighting was long and fierce. Arnór Jarlaskáld says :

> "'Once, off Dyrness, to the eastward,
> Came King Kali in a mail-coat
> Famous for its strength and brightness ;
> But the land was not defenceless,
> For, with five ships, nothing daunted,
> Scorning flight in warlike temper,
> Valiantly the Prince went forward
> 'Gainst the King's eleven vessels.

> "'Then the ships were lashed together—
> Know ye how the men were falling?
> All their swords and boards were swimming
> In the life-blood of the Scotsmen;
> Hearts were sinking—bowstrings screaming,
> Darts were flying—spear-shafts bending;
> Swords were biting, blood flowed freely,
> And the Prince's heart was merry.'

"Now Earl Thorfinn incited his men to the utmost, and a fierce conflict ensued. The Scots in the King's ships made but a feeble resistance before the mast, whereupon Thorfinn jumped from the quarter-deck, and ran to the fore-deck and fought fiercely. When he saw the crowd in the King's ships getting thinner, he urged his men to board them. King Karl, perceiving this, gave orders to his men to cut the ropes, and get the ships away instantly; to take to their oars, and bear away. At the same time Thorfinn and his men fastened grappling-hooks in the King's ship. He called for his banner to be borne before him, and a great number of his men followed it. King Karl jumped from his ship into another vessel, with those of his men who still held out; but the most part had fallen already. He then ordered them to take to their oars; and the Scots took to flight—Thorfinn pursuing them. Thus says Arnór:

> "'Never was a battle shorter;
> Soon with spears it was decided.
> Though my lord had fewer numbers,
> Yet he chased them all before him;
> Hoarsely croaked the battle-gull, when
> Thickly fell the wounded king's-men;
> South of Sandwick swords were reddened.'"

Leaving Sandside, a quarter of an hour's walk brings us to the Gloup of Deerness, which is a wild, gruesome looking place. It is a vast chasm in the land, nearly 80 yards long, and half as broad, and perhaps 100 feet in depth. Standing at the side, the waves are seen dashing in in wildest fury, through a long channel communicating with the sea.

Another short walk brings us to the Brough of Deerness, which at high tide is almost insulated. The course to the Brough is not an easy one—large boulders having to be got over; and the path to the top of the rock is narrow and not free of danger, unless to those possessed of a good nerve. About the centre of the Brough there is the remains of an old chapel, which will be found fully described in Appendix A.

Jo Ben, writing on this chapel in 1529, describes it as "the Bairns of Burgh," and it appears from this account that it was a place of pilgrimage. On hands and knees the pilgrims are said to have clambered to the top of the path, one at a time. With bent knees and hands clasped, they then went round the chapel three times, appealing to the Bairns of Burgh, and at intervals threw stones and water behind them.

If we cross over to the west side of the Moul Head, to Scarvating, we will there have pointed out to us the graves of many martyrs, who perished off here in December, 1679. After the disastrous battle of Bothwell Bridge, 1,200 Covenanters were taken prisoners, and 257 of these were put on board the ship Crown, at Leith (which was under the command of one Paterson a Papist), on the 15th November, 1679. "There the two hundred and fifty-seven were stowed into a place hardly capable of containing a hundred persons, so closely packed that the greater part were obliged to stand, in order to make room for their sick and dying companions to stretch themselves; many of them fainted, or were suffocated from want of air; and the seamen, as if the spirit of persecution had infected their usually generous natures, treated them with cruelty too shocking to be described. At length the vessel was overtaken by a storm on the coast of Orkney, and foundered on the rocks. All might have easily escaped; but, after securing the crew, the inhuman captain ordered the hatches to be locked upon the prisoners. Some forty or fifty contrived to save themselves by clinging to the boards of the ship, but two hundred met with a watery grave. The wretch who was guilty of this cold-blooded murder was never called to account. But the fate of those who perished was merciful, when compared with that of their companions who escaped this martyrdom. These were banished as slaves to the plantations in Jamaica and New Jersey, where they were compelled to labour under a burning sun, in the same gang with the negroes; and of two hundred and sixty who were so disposed of at different times during the persecution, very

few remained to be released from their bondage at the Revolution."
On the farm of Milldam, some interesting ruins were found in the
summer of 1861. They stand on a slope of a low hill near the farm.
Beneath the surface of the soil were numerous traces of ancient buildings, and remains of stone-vessels similar to those which are often
found in the "Broughs" or large round Towers. Also a stone so
deeply notched at one end, that when the other, which is very thick,
is fixed in the ground, it forms a strong stake. It was of a wedge
shape, the notches being at the thin end, and the thick end having
been evidently intended to be inserted in the ground. Similar stones
have been frequently found in the Burgs, and in the neighbourhood
of the ruins. In some cases the notches or grooves have been much
worn by a rope or other fastening. On the summit of the hill were
two "barrows" or grave mounds. The barrows contained several
kists (kistavens) or graves of various sizes, in which were quantities
of burnt bones; and two rudely fashioned clay urns, also containing
burnt bones, were found outside the kists.

Eleven kists are understood to have been found in the barrow.
One about the centre of the barrow, and on a level with the surrounding soil, was formed by flagstones set on edge, neatly fitted at the
angles, and the cover, which was considerably larger than the mouth
of the kist, had been roughly dressed. A large block of stone,
nearly 5 feet long, 4 feet broad, and 7 inches thick, lay over the
cover of the kist. The other graves or kists, which were more
rudely formed, seemed to have been placed around this centre one,
but on a different level—their bottoms being on a level with the
top of the centre kist. Three of these were on the west side of the
barrow. One was 3 feet in length and breadth, and about $2\frac{1}{4}$ feet
in depth, and contained a smaller one about a foot square. The
burnt bones in this case were in the smaller kist. The adjoining
kist was somewhat narrower, and the third kist was still smaller.
They both contained burnt bones. A portion of a lower jawbone
and fragments of a collar bone proved that they belonged to a
human skeleton.

On the farm of Newhall, some ancient ruins were also found in

June, 1864, concealed beneath a grassy hillock. It appears as if there had been a large building on the spot, but so completely has it been destroyed that no idea can now be formed of its size or form. The great quantities of bones of animals and shells of whelks, limpets, and other shell fish, and the thick layers of ashes in which they are embedded, show that the building had long been occupied as a dwelling, while the horns and *bones of deers*, rude pottery, and many fragments of stone vessels, prove its great antiquity. The articles found consisted of a flat piece of a jaw bone of a whale, about 13 inches long, and $2\frac{1}{2}$ inches broad, with two holes through it, and indications of other two at its ends; fragments of a bone comb, rudely adorned with small incised circles, and fastened together with iron pins; a fragment of a small clay vessel; a "whorl" or bead of burnt clay; fragments of deers' horns, one piece evidently of a very large horn; and a large boar's tusk. In addition to these there have been found a rude stone vessel, about 21 inches long, 10 inches broad, and 6 to 7 inches thick (the cavity in it 1 foot long, 6 inches wide, and only 2 inches deep); a fragment of a quern stone, which had probably been about 18 inches in diameter; half of a small quern stone about 9 inches in diameter; another stone, nearly square, but having the corners rounded off; two other stones, which have had cavities near the centre about $4\frac{1}{2}$ inches in diameter, and $2\frac{1}{4}$ inches deep; a spherical stone, which has been apparently used as a grinder or crusher; several pieces of pottery, one of the fragments well formed and very smooth; another piece with remains of glazing on it, and several pieces very coarse and scored or incised in a very primitive manner; the primitive and the more artistic relics were found lying close together. The handle, unquestionably of a spoon made from a bone of some animal, was also picked up in the *debris*.

Seating ourselves in our conveyance, we now drive back towards Kirkwall, till we approach the Public School at Brough, when we take the road to the left. The country here is bleak and wild, there being a large stretch of heather. A smart drive brings us into the parish of

Holm,

Which lies to the south-east of Kirkwall. Before we turn into the village, we pass, on the right, the fine mansion-house of Græmeshall, the residence of the principal proprietor of the parish.

A stirring incident took place here in the month of June, 1694. At that time, when Alexander Cleat, tenant in Henbuster, was out at sea with three companions in a boat fishing, to the eastward of the parish of Holm, two French Privateers, which were cruising in the offing, bore down upon them, and Robert Dunbar, captain of one of the "frigates," compelled Cleat and the other boatmen to go on board and pilot the vessels into Holm Sound. On their arrival in the Sound, the Privateers first seized three vessels which were lying at anchor, and then sent the "long-boats" full of armed men to the Island of Lambholm, "notwithstanding that James Graham of Grahamshall did fire several cannon shots at the boats," as they passed from the ships to the Island. On landing they collected all the "kyne, bulls, sheep, swine, geese, and other small store," together with the "whole bere, meal, malt, butter, and also house plenishing such as beds, bedding, pots, pans, woollen and linen webs, and linen and woollen yarn and fishing lines." "What bere, meal, and malt they could not carry away, they threw over the rocks into the sea, or sowed amongst the stones on the shore." They sank the fishing boat of the Isle, and, cutting the fastenings of the horses, turned them into the growing corn, which they also maliciously trampled under foot. Two bulls and a cow were killed before they were put into the boat, and the plunderers then returned to their ships laden with booty.

Their next exploit was to land a boat filled with armed men at the storehouse of Græmeshall—the same which may yet be seen to the eastward of the village of St Mary's. Their proceedings were watched at a very respectful distance by Nicol Anderson, tenant in Ackerbuster, who stated at his examination before the Sheriff that they broke open the door, which had two locks upon it, but he could not see what they carried away with them.

The alarm soon spread through the parish. The beacon fires were lighted on the Wart (Ward) hills, and were repeated from hill to hill, and a force variously computed at from 400 to 600 men was speedily collected from the parishes of Deerness, St Andrews, St Ola, and Holm, and the town of Kirkwall, and assembled at the house of Græmeshall, where they were entertained four days by Mr Græme. The French, deterred by their presence, did not again attempt to land, but, on the third day, got their ships under sail and proceeded out to sea, having previously thrown some of the living cattle overboard.

The damage done on that occasion must have been considerable, for Magnus Bews, in Swartaquoy, who was in Lambholm when the French landed there, estimated the loss sustained by Mr Græme by the plunder of Lambholm, at upwards of £1000 Scots, exclusive of the expenses he incurred in entertaining several hundred men at his house for four days.

Scattered over the parish are a large number of mounds. There are also two fine lochs here—Græmeshall and St Mary's—but permission to fish in them must be got from Mr Græme. About three miles south of the village, at Roseness Point, the rock scenery is very wild, and a large gloup there will well repay a visit.

We now send our conveyance on to Kirkwall, whilst we proceed to the island of

Burray.

This island is separated from Holm by Holm Sound, which is about three miles broad. Boatmen will carry us across for about 2s, and will land us within easy distance of a large and important Burg.

The name given to the island in the old Sagas, is " Borgar-ey " or the Burg Isle, evidently showing that the Burg or Brugh existed (perhaps in ruins) when the Norwegians invaded Orkney, but that at all events it was so conspicuous an object that they named the island after it. It has been an immense pile of building—66 ft. in diameter—the inclosed area being 36 feet, and the wall 15 feet across. A ledge of projecting stones running round the inside of the wall at about 11 feet from the floor, and slanting upwards,

G

suggest the idea of some sort of roof being rested on the ledge to shelter the area beneath. Immediately above the ledge the walls recede about 6 inches, and rise to an additional height in some places of 5 or 6 feet; but that the original height of the building must have been at least 30 feet, may be inferred from the vast quantity of stones which were lying within and around the walls. There is only one entrance to the building; it is on the east side, and appears to have been very effectually guarded by a cell on each side in the thickness of the wall, with low entrances, 3 feet in height, opening into the passage or doorway. Had an enemy got about two-thirds through the passage he would find a barricade of large upright flags stopping his farther progress, and at the same time each leg would be seized by invisible foes concealed in the cells on each hand, and ere he could extricate himself he would be despatched by weapons thrust through between the lintels overhead, for there is a deep recess in the wall above and parallel with the passage, in which several men could stand in concealment, and use their weapons effectually on any hapless assailant of their stronghold who ventured into the passage beneath. There is another cell in the wall opposite to the inner opening of the passage, and two others about 5 feet from the ground, one on the north and the other on the south side, all opening on the area. Probably there were other cells higher up. We believe there is enough of stones in the ruins to build a dyke 5 feet high, 18 inches broad, and nearly two miles long.

The Burg was defended on the land side by an embankment of earth, and had a well attached to it by a concealed passage. Among the articles found in the ruins were stone vessels, a stone lamp, several portions of stone querns, stone beads, a rudely formed baked clay cup, combs and pins of bone, part of a bone wheel which had been about 10 inches in diameter, and made out of the jaw bone, and a cup, of the vertebre of a whale, bone heads, a bronze pin, and various implements of iron, in short, a collection embracing specimens from each of the stone, bronze, and iron periods; and thus satis-factorily proving that while buildings which contain bronze and iron have been erected during the stone period, they do not necessarily belong to the latter periods of bronze and iron. We are inclined to infer from the relics of the three periods being found in the same building, that there was no gradual transition in Orkney from stone to bronze, and from bronze to iron ; but that the building in Burray and others of its class were erected by a race unacquainted with metals, and therefore using stone and bone implements, and that they were invaded and supplanted by a race higher in the scale of civilization, who brought along with them ornaments of bronze and probably weapons of iron. A similar intermixture of the relics of the several periods have been observed in other Burgs in Orkney, and we may therefore conclude that it was at the commencement of the iron period, when bronze was still much in use, that the race which built these Burgs, and used only stone and bone implements, were supplanted by another race, who brought with them bronze and iron, and hence the intermixture of the relics of the different periods. It is just similar to what we would expect to find in the dwelling of one of the aborigines of Australia, were it suddenly to become a ruin, and after a lapse of time to be examined. The rude implements of the aboriginal inhabitant would be found lying side by side with the highly finished metallic implements introduced by the Saxon invader of his territory.

At a little distance from the wall on the north side of the inclosed area of the Burg, a small quantity of charred bere was found lying embedded in clay, and mixed with charred wood. It lay beneath the whole of the stones and rubbish which had fallen within the building, and must have been placed there before the Burg had become a total ruin. It was evidently meant to have been roasted, but had got rather more of the fire than was intended. Perhaps in the last siege of the Burg one of its occupants had been sitting roasting the bere preparatory to rubbing or bruising it in one of the stone mortars found in the ruins, or grinding it in the quern, when he was suddenly called to assist in the defence of the castle, and the bere was left to become charred, as it was found. We here get a glimpse of the mode in which the grain was prepared by the early inhabitants of Orkney. One cannot help here reminded of the "*Burstein*" formerly so common in the north isles, and which we have no doubt was just what the old fellow in the Burray Burg was preparing when he had to leave it as a legacy to us, and betake himself to more perilous employment.

We now walk across the island to Watersound, where, for a sixpence, we will get a boat to land us at

South Ronaldshay.

Here there is a large village—St Margaret's Hope—which has always a busy appearance—especially during the herring fishing season.

In this island there are three chapels commemorative of St Columbian, at Grymness, Hoxay, and Loch of Burwick. At Stoose, St Ninian was commemorated. The other chapels were—St Andrews, at Windwick; Our Lady, at Halcro; the Reind, at Sandwick; St Tola, at Widewall; and Margaret, at St Margaret's Hope.

A walk of about half an hour from the village brings us to the vicinity of Hoxa Head, where there is the remains of a Burg, which was opened up by the late Mr Petrie, in 1848. The diameter inside was about 30 ft., and the thickness of the outer wall 13 ft. On the western side a wall 10 ft. high and 1 ft. thick had been built. Some stone troughs, and six stone querns were found here. On the eastern side is the doorway. Near this, there are several other mounds, which have not, however, been opened up.

On the east side, near the parish manse, there is a standing stone, 16 ft. high.

We now proceed to the south parish, and as we near our destination we get some fine views of the Pentland Firth. Here we pass Tomison's Acadamy, endowed by an old Hudson Bay trader, named Wm. Tomison. It is seated to accommodate 600 scholars, who get a high-class education free of charge.

At the Parish Church at Burwick, "is to be seen a curious boat-shaped stone, some four feet long, two broad in the centre, and eight inches thick, on which are clearly impressed the marks of two naked feet. Low suggests that it was used as a stone, upon which delinquents were made to stand in Roman Catholic days."

In the churchyards on this island there are some very quaint tombstone inscriptions. Here is one taken from the Churchyard of St Peter's :—

" Heir lyes a very onest
woman caled Caitrin
Groat and spous to
Donald Robson skipr
depairtit the 4 of
November 1643.
Heir rests this corps
Enclosed in clay
As al must doeis
At the last day."

The following inscription will also be found in the same graveyard :—

" Sacred to the memory of Robert
Robinson who departed this
Life Jany. 22, 1728, aged 21.
Here lyes a youthful hardy tar
Life's troubled ocean past,
Thro' storms and loud alarms of war
He's anchored here at last.
From dread of seas and adverse winds
His sheltered bark's secure,
For here serenest calms he finds
Forever to endure.
But once more he must rear his head
With many of the fleet,
His anchor weigh, his canvas spread,
His Admiral Christ to meet."

When in the south parish, a visit should be paid to the Gloup of Halcro, which is indeed a wild looking chasm, and must be over 100 feet in depth. It is said that the tunnel which connects the gloup with the sea, can be explored by a small boat ; but the undertaking, we fancy, would not be a pleasant one.

Having now " done" South Ronaldshay, we will proceed to the Howe of Hoxa, where we will catch the mail steamer about 11 p.m., and should reach Scapa (Kirkwall), a little after midnight.

AN EXCURSION TO THE NORTH ISLES.

A TRIP to the North Isles is always very enjoyable in the summer season. There are so many features of general interest in the islands, the rock scenery is so grand, whilst the sea breezes are so fresh and invigorating, that nothing could be more pleasant than roving at one's free will

> " Far from the busy haunts of men,
> Far from the heartless multitude."

Every afternoon (Sunday excepted) a substantial packet leaves Kirkwall for Shapinsay, or, if the tourist prefers, he can hire a small boat, for a few shillings, to take him there. With a favourable breeze, a sail of a little over half-an-hour will carry us to

Shapinsay,

Which is the property of Colonel Balfour, of Balfour and Trenabie. Landing at the village, a few minutes' walk brings us to the chief attraction in the island, Balfour Castle, which is built upon the site of the former family mansion, Cliffdale. Balfour Castle is the best and largest specimen of architecture in the county, and always calls forth the admiration of visitors to the islands. The grounds around the Castle, about fifty acres in extent, are laid out with great taste— the gardens and plantations being most attractive.

Balfour Village, which faces the harbour, is a snug little place, each house having a nice garden plot in front.

Leaving the village we proceed along the public road, which runs through the centre of the island. As we pass along we will have no difficulty in finding Mooro's Stone, which is not unlike the Standing

Stones of Stennis. On one side of it there are four marks, and on the other one mark. Tradition says these are the finger marks of a giant named Mooro, who hurled it at some enemy in Eday, but not having sufficient force, it fell here.

BALFOUR CASTLE—SHAPINSAY.

We now pass along to the Burg of " Borrowston." The wall of this interesting Burg has probably been originally quite circular, but has evidently been rebuilt and faced up in various places, so that it is now far from symmetrical. It is about twelve feet thick, and at present between thirteen and fourteen feet high. The enclosed area has an average diameter of about thirty-one feet. The entrance or doorway is in the direction of E.S.E. The doorway has been extended outwards about 6½ feet (probably at a date long subsequent to the original erection of the Burg) and then branches into two narrow passages which appear to terminate immediately above the beach. A short passage 2¾ ft. high and 20 inches wide, in the south side of the doorway, is the entrance to a chamber or gallery which is 7½ feet high, and 5 feet wide next the entrance, and follows the curve of the wall for about 12 feet, when its inner extremity, which is there low and narrow, appears to be choked with rubbish. A concentric wall from 2 to 3 feet thick, with a space of about 6 feet between it and the principal wall of the Burg occupies a considerable portion of the area on the side opposite to the door. The intervening space between those concentric walls was most probably all roofed over with flagstones, forming a gallery or series of chambers, of which the roofing and ruined chamber at the south side are the remains. As in the Burray Burg a ledge about 18 inches broad runs round the wall in the interior, 10 or 11 feet above the floor; and nearly on the level of the ledge there are two openings or doorways in the wall, one opposite to the principal entrance, and the other on the south side. The latter is 2 feet 8 inches long, and forms an entrance to a gallery 2¾ feet wide in the thickness of the wall. In the floor of the area opposite the doorway, and within a couple of feet of the fragmentary wall there is a hole of an irregular figure about 4 feet one way, and 2 another, and about 10 feet deep. The bottom is excavated in the rock, and the sides are built in the rudest manner. A similar cell or cavity is almost invariably found in, or adjacent to, each Burg. It has been customary to assume these to have been wells, and, as is too generally the case in antiquarian researches, it has been taken for granted that every subsequent discovery connected with them has pointed in the same direction. There are, however, many objections to such a theory which it is unnecessary here to state, while there are many reasons for believing that the so-called wells were just the "safes" in which the inhabitants of the Burgs concealed and secured their treasures in times of danger.

The Burg appears to be surrounded at a distance of 9 feet by a stone wall 3¼ feet thick, and outside this wall is a wide and deep trench, and an earthen rampart inclosing the whole. The entire diameter of the Burg and its outworks is about 170 feet.

That the Orkney Burgs belong to a period prior to the Scandinavian invasion of the islands is certain, but by what race of people they were erected remains to be discovered. Taken, however, in connection with other remains existing in the islands, they furnish pretty conclusive evidence that the Norsemen had been preceded in Orkney by a population who looked upon the islands as a permanent residence, and had attained a considerable degree of civilization. One proof of this is the fact that ruins of several ancient mills have been discovered in Shapinsay. Under the ancient Norwegian laws such mills would not have been tolerated, nor could they have been erected since the island came under the Scotch rule; and as these ruins bear every mark of great antiquity, they must be traced to a race antecedent to the Norse colonists.

URN FOUND AT SHAPINSAY.

On the north-east shore is the remains of Linton Chapel, which is more fully described in Appendix A.

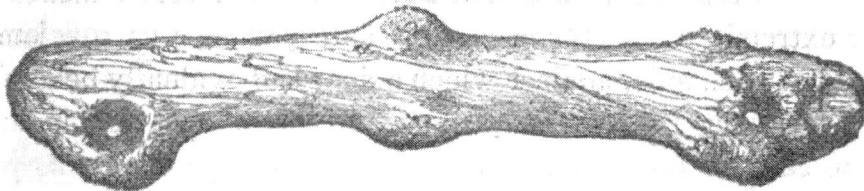

YOKE FOR OXEN FOUND AT SHAPINSAY.

When in this part of the island the coast scenery should be visited.

There are many fine natural arches, and beautiful geos, which run hundreds of yards into the island. Sea-fowl are always to be found here in large numbers, and rock pigeons breed very extensively in crevices of the cliffs.

On the island there is an old stone wall, partially covered with moss, which always proves of interest to the antiquary.

The North Isles steamer leaves Kirkwall every Wednesday and Saturday—the hours for sailing varying to suit the tides; but the monthly time-table is always published in the *Orcadian* newspaper. Supposing we have made our visit to Shapinsay on a Tuesday or a Friday, next morning we should hire a small boat, and go out into the course of the steamer, and get on board as it is passing the island, and proceed to

Stronsay.

On our way thither the scenery is very fine. As we pass Ness Point, the Islands of Shapinsay and Stronsay seem to join. In the days before steam was introduced, and when the North Isles people came in to Kirkwall in large numbers with sailing craft, when they reached this point they held high revel—whisky bottles and bread and cheese being produced in great abundance.

The steamer stops at Whitehall Pier, which is built in the bay of that name, at the north end of the island. Here there is a large and thriving village, which, owing to the great and increasing activity in the herring fishing, is growing in importance yearly.

If we take the public road at the pier, a nice walk up hill brings us to Hunton. Here there is a ruined Burg. It was examined in 1863. The passage was about 5 feet high, and $2\frac{1}{2}$ feet wide at its outer entrance; and extending inwards $13\frac{1}{2}$ feet, widening in the middle to 3 feet 10 inches, and narrowing to 2 feet 7 inches at the inner extremity. Rather more than half way in, a narrow jamb was formed at each side, against which a door had evidently been placed; two holes being in the wall on each side to keep the door in its place, and to bar out intruders. The length of the passage was just the thickness of the wall of the burg which had been thrown down, the ruins of the wall blocking up the inner end of the passage. The whole diameter of the tower had been from 60 to 65 feet, but there had been besides a great extent of outworks, and the whole of the large mound in which the discovery has been made, is a mass of ruins.

We now pass along to the extreme south end, to Lamb Head, where we will see the remains of another burg, in the walls of which many cells were found. Near here there is a wild geo, known to the natives as "Hell's Mouth." Striking out now for the Vat of Kirbister, we come to to the Geo of Odin, the sides of which are covered with dulse. The people of Stronsay have an old proverb regarding this species of sea weed. It is—" The Well of Kildinguie, and the dulse of Geo Odin will cure all diseases but Black Death." This famous well is in the Mill Bay, and though it is covered at high water, when the tide recedes, the brackishness goes with it. The well is said to have been, in former times, a great resort for pilgrims, and a stone bench is pointed out on the south side of it, on which the officiating priest sat, whilst in front of it there is a mark in the rock, said to have been caused by the priest's feet. The Vat of Kirbister has the circular-like appearance of a vast basin, nearly eighty yards in diameter, and one hundred feet in height. There is a magnificent rock arch on the eastern side, whilst inside there are three fine caves.

Having finished our tour round Stronsay, a boat should now be hired to carry us across the three miles of sea which separates this island from

Sanday.

The area of this island is nineteen square miles. It is divided into two parishes, namely, the united parishes of Cross and Burness and Lady Parish. There are two harbours—Kettletoft on the south, and Otterswick on the north-east. Of late years the island has made great advances in agriculture, and there is now very little waste land.

The island lies low, and before the erection of the Start Light-house, in hazy or stormy weather, was the scene of many wrecks. It is related that once when Stevenson, the well-known lighthouse

engineer, drew the attention of a Sanday farmer to the bad condition
of the sails of his boat, the farmer retorted—"If it had been His
(*i.e.* God's) will, that you had na built sae many lighthouses here-
about, I would have had new sails last winter." It is also said that
a Sanday minister prayed—" Nevertheless, if it please Thee to cause
helpless ships to be cast on the shore, oh! dinna forget the poor
island of Sanday!"

There are few antiquarian remains in the island. The most
important is at Elsness. It is a large mound, which was examined
in 1867, by Mr Farrer, M.P., who communicated the result as follows,
to the *Orcadian* of August 6, 1867:—" Quoy Ness in Elsness, Isle
of Sanday, presents the usual appearance of a large brough. It is
close to the sea, and only a few feet above high water mark. The
diameter of the mound, in its present ruined condition is 63 ft., and
$12\frac{1}{2}$ ft. in height. From the vast quantities of debris, it may be
inferred that when originally constructed, it must have been very
much higher. The diameter of the building in which the graves or
kists are found is 32 ft. The space between the inner wall and the
outer one is 12 ft., and seems to have been an area or court, probably
encircling the whole building. This area is now completely filled
with rubbish, and the outer wall itself shows symptoms of decay.
Outside of this wall another appears, the stones being laid with
great regularity on the outside, but the interior—$3\frac{1}{2}$ ft.—is filled up
with loose stones, the object probably having been to strengthen
the original wall. On the south-east side of the mound there is a
passage, 12 ft. long, and 21 in. wide, covered with large stones set
on edge. Here several human skulls—apparently of a very low
type, were found—they were in a decayed state. A stratum of
decayed bones was cut through, but very few of them were in a
sufficiently sound state to bear lifting. Some of the skulls are of
great thickness—a fragment of one was at least half an inch thick.
This passage was paved with flat stones. Entering the building, it
continues a further distance of 12 ft., and was partially filled up with
stone and earthy matter. Like the one outside, it is covered over
with large stones set on edge. One of these stones had fallen in,

and there were appearances of an upper tier of similar stones. The passage is 3 ft. in height, and 21 in. wide, and is unpaved. When cleared out, it proved to communicate with a large oblong chamber in the centre of the mound. This chamber is 11 ft. 10 in. long, 4 ft. 6 in. wide, and 12 ft. 6 in. deep. Within the wall, on the north-west side, are two kists of a semicircular shape, 19 in. wide at the entrance, and 6 ft. high in the inside and 5 ft., respectively. They contained no bones. On the right of the entrance passage there is a kist, 20 in. wide, and 6 ft. high, and on the left another, probably of the same dimensions, but not yet cleared out. Both of these kists contained skulls, and a few other human bones. In the angle formed by the south-east and south-west walls, is a small circular kist sunk in the ground, 2 ft. in diameter, and containing some human leg and arm bones in the last stage of decay. On the south-west side is a kist, 5 ft. high, and 2 ft. wide at the entrance, and on the north-east side one pear-shaped, in which human remains were discovered. Many of the teeth were perfect, still preserving the enamel—others bore evidence to the fact that these ancient people had no immunity from toothache. A battle axe of basalt (I believe), a bone dagger about 7 in. long, and worked stone for pounding corn, were the only things of an artificial character discovered amongst the rubbish. The skulls and jaw-bones (which I propose to forward to Dr Thurnam, the well-known craniologist), are of various sizes ; but owing to the very decayed state of all the bones, it is difficult to estimate the probable stature of the individuals to whom they belonged. One thigh-bone was $17\frac{1}{2}$ inches long, and in good preservation, but it may be doubted whether this does not belong to some later interment. I am disposed to think that until further investigation has been made, it would be difficult to determine positively whether the mound was in its *original* state a burial place. It *may* have been a brough, and the space between the inner and outer walls—which I suppose to have been an open area—may in reality have been a mass of rude walling, constructed with a view of supporting the building in which the graves are found. Further excavations can alone settle this point. I may take this opportunity of expressing my thanks to Mr Ross, road contractor, and Mr Learmonth of Elsness, for the assistance that they rendered me in opening out this curious relic of past ages. Quoy Ness is on the property of Geo. Traill, Esq., M.P., who kindly gave me leave to make excavations on his estates in Orkney some years ago."

At the south end of the island there is a curious conglomerate formation of rock at Hecklabor. In the Burness parish, at Saville, there is a large boulder of gneiss. Near the Manse of Cross and Burness there is an interesting cave called Helziegio, which, however, can only be approached in fine weather; and many curious stratifications, interesting to the geologist, may be seen on different parts of the coast.

We now proceed to Otterswick Bay, where the mail boat leaves every Wednesday for

North Ronaldshay.

The Sound of North Ronaldshay is about five miles broad, and the time occupied in crossing it in fair weather varies from forty minutes to an hour. The island, which is about five miles in length, and three in breadth, is the most northerly in the Orcadian group, and around it stretches the Atlantic and German Oceans. The island contains about 2000 acres, and is mostly divided into small farms. Though somewhat remote, it may be called a " gem of the ocean." The soil for the most part is very fertile, and produces excellent crops.

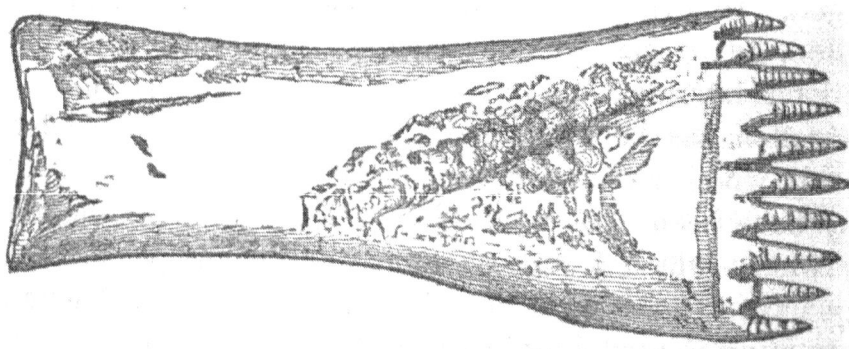

COMB FOUND IN THE BURG AT BURRIAN.

The first thing that strikes the visitor, is the wall which runs round the entire island. Outside this enclosure the sheep roam all winter, feeding on sea-ware, and are very nimble amongst the rocks and boulders.

Holland House, the residence of Dr Traill, the proprietor of the island, is situated upon the highest point in the island. At the south end is the Burg of Burrian, which was opened up by Dr Traill in 1870. In it some runic inscriptions were found, a small Celtic ecclesiastical bell, an ornamented ox-bone, and stones with incised triangles. A large number of bone implements were also found, amongst these being some well-formed combs, of which we give illustrations.

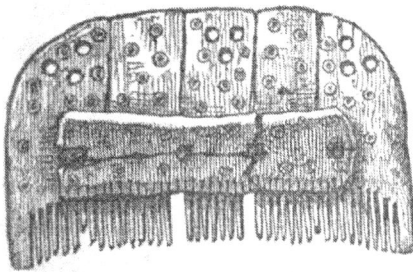

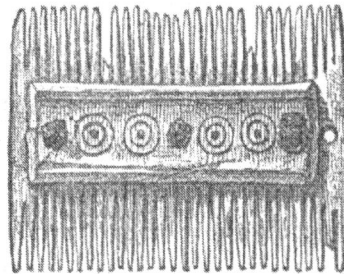

COMBS FOUND IN THE BURG OF BURRIAN.

North of Dennis Head is Seal Skerry, so called from the large numbers of seals which are usually to be found there. Jo Ben states that he himself saw no less that sixty captured there with a net at one time.

At the north end of the island there is a magnificent lighthouse, said to be the second best in the kingdom, from which a grand view can be had of the surrounding sea and islands.

If the visitor does not care to remain here till the next mail day a boat can be hired to go across to

Westray.

This is the largest of the North Isles. At the Bay of Pierowall where the steamer calls, there is a large village. On the island there are many attractions for the antiquarian. During the Viking period, the Norsemen often met here, and have left many traces of their presence. From time to time many relics have been found on the island.   An oval brooch of which the accompanying is a correct wood-cut, was found in Westray a few years ago.

OVAL BOWL BROOCH FOUND IN A VIKING GRAVE AT WESTRAY.

In 1860 a large number of human skeletons were discovered on the farm of Breck-o'-wall, at the house of Knockerhall.   They were contained in two large graves or tombs, each about ten feet long and eight feet wide.   Large stones set on edge formed the west side, and a large block of stone eight feet wide and one foot thick, and a small piece of rudely built wall shut in the west side.   The skeletons were ranged in five or six tiers, one above the other, the skulls in one tier being placed north, and in the other south alternately.   Some of the skeletons were in a bent or flexed position, and others lay on their sides, and the graves were filled up with stones which appeared to have been carefully thrown in.   The probability is that these skeletons are the remains of some of the early inhabitants of Westray, who had been slain in battle, for the general appearance of the graves and their contents leave little doubt that the bodies were all interred at one and the same time.

A stone ball, about three inches in diameter, was found beside the skeletons.   It was, with great labour, rubbed down to a spherical form, and closely resembled similar stones which have been found in ancient graves in other parts of Scotland.

On the north links of Westray there are two ancient dwellings. One of them has been explored.   It is a single chamber communicating with the surface by a short steep passage two and a-half feet high.   The roof of the chamber is of large flags supported on the walls and on blocks of stone and rudely built pillars. A knocking stone, was the only relic found in it, but it was sufficient to show that the building was used as a dwelling. A shard or heap of sand sixteen feet high, with grass on its top, still remains to show that since the chamber was built the sand had accumulated to that height above it, and again been removed by the storms of long centuries.

We now make straight past the village of Pierowall for Noltland Castle, which, independent of its magnificent architecture, has a history that reads like romance. It is built in the form of a parallelogram, measures 86 ft. 10 in. E. and W., and 36 ft. 3 in. N. and S., with rectangular towers at the S.W. and N.E. corners. " A good notion of its dimensions may be formed from the fact of the central column, or newel, being nearly one yard in diameter. The destruction of its pyramidal terminal is much to be regretted, for this staircase is perfectly unique, especially the guardroom at its summit; here, supposing an enemy to have gained possession of the stairs, and about entering in fancied safety, he would have to encounter the aim of hidden foes, whose fire would be directed from the shot-hole behind the central column."

Owing to the numerous port holes in the building, there is a prevalent belief that the architect was a sailor, and tradition has it that his remains are interred in the staircase of the south-western tower. The erection of the Castle was commenced somewhere about the year 1422, by Thomas de Tulloch, then Bishop of Orkney, and his initals, T. T., with the figure of a bishop in a kneeling posture, was for a long time an attractive ornament of the pillar supporting the grand staircase.

Noltland Castle had a chequered career. About the end of the fifteenth century it was besieged and taken possession of by Sir William Sinclair, of Warsetter. It was next stormed by Earl Patrick Stewart, and its inmates taken prisoners to Kirkwall.

"Its last Episcopal possessor was the well-known Adam Bothwell, Bishop of Orkney, who gifted it over to his brother-in-law, Sir Gilbert Balfour, Master of Queen Mary's Household, Sheriff of

Orkney, and Captain of Kirkwall Castle. It is thus that the confusion of Balfour's connection with *Bishop* Bothwell and *Earl* Bothwell has arisen, and been repeated by one writer after another, until it actually came to be believed that Sir Gilbert built Noltland Castle as a refuge for the husband of the unfortunate Mary, the infamous Duke of Orkney!"

The owners of the Castle were continually getting into trouble. Sir Gilbert Balfour, who had received orders to prepare it in preparation for Queen Mary, upon her escape from Lochleven Castle, was exiled, and his estates forfeited. For sheltering officers of Montrose's army, after the disastrous defeat at Corbiesdale, Sir Patrick Balfour, then owner of Noltland Castle, had to fly the country.

After the rebellion of 1745, this old historical building was deprived of its roof, and was never afterwards inhabited. It seems that Wm. Balfour had taken an active part with the Jacobites in these stirring times, and as a punishment, the Hanoverians, it is said, fired Noltland Castle, which has been roofless ever since.

About a quarter of an hour's walk from the Castle we arrive at the Gentlemen's Ha', which is a large Cave in the face of the cliffs. The ledge of rock which leads down to it is broken, and a chasm nearly a yard wide has to be jumped before the Cave can be reached. The leap is not at all a pleasant one, with the sea rumbling and tumbling about one hundred feet beneath you. The Gentlemen's Ha' got its name from the fact that five Jacobite gentlemen—Balfour of Trenaby, Traill of Elsness, Traill of Westness, Stewart of Brough, and Coventry of Newark—hid themselves here for a whole winter, after the disastrous defeat of Prince Charles at Culloden.

Another ten minutes' walk brings us to Ramna Geo, where there is a cave which runs right through to the other side of the headland. We are now at Noup Head, which is nearly 250 feet high, and it is beautifully terraced. The rock scenery here is grand, and always calls forth the admiration of those who visit it, whilst from the Head itself a splendid view is to be had of part of the west mainland, Hoy, and the north isles.

If the tourist cares to spend a day in Westray, he can get good angling in Saint Ear and Burness lochs (above the village of Pierowall), where the trout is of good size, and fairly plentiful. When here a short walk will take us to Fitty Hill, from which a fine view can be had of the surrounding islands.

We now hire a small boat to take us across to

Papa Westray,

Which lies north-east of Westray, and is owned by Thos. Traill, Esq., of Holland. The island is about three and a half miles long, and one broad. Upon landing about the middle of the west side of the island, we see a long stretch of beach, the many boulders on which makes it a very suitable place for drying the hundreds of tons of fish which are annually cured here. About 60 yards above the landing place, strangers can have refreshments, and, if necessary, private lodgings. The beach northwards is very pretty. A quarter of an hour's walk brings us to the old Established Church and grave yard. Down on the shore below this, there is a large pictshouse. About the middle of the north side are the geos or caves, called the Ha's, and from the hill above can be seen the whole fishing ground, as well as the wild Bore Roost. The rocks on the north-easterly side are swarming with sea-fowl, and along the east there is a very nice white beach, and some pretty little bays.

Near the middle of the island, stands the mansion house of Holland, the residence of the proprietor, Mr Traill, "the head of all the Orcadian and Caithness families of that name." Over the old house of Holland was the following lines, which will give an idea of the hospitality of the old Orcadian families :—

> " Come good folk and make good cheer ;
> All civil people are welcome here,
> And only for a good man's sake,
> What God doth send ; ye shall not lack ;
> For good he was to me indeed,
> Forward then his name ye read,
> "T. T. & M. C., 1632."

This now forms the back of one of the lobby chairs in the present mansion house.

A very pretty loch stretches across almost half the length of the island. On its eastern margin there is a flat projecting point, on which towers a large pile of ruins covered with grass, with the exception of a few large stones. Pitched on the summit of this heap are the crumbling walls of a building that bears marks of considerable antiquity, although erected at a date long posterior to the pictshouse or burg on whose ruins it stands. There is little to draw attention to the building now, but half a century ago, and perhaps much later, it was a centre of attraction not only to the inhabitants of Papa Westray, but also to those of the neighbouring islands. Then there might have been seen toiling up to the tottering fabric, those who were the victims of incurable diseases, crawling thither in the vain expectation that when every other means had proved ineffectual, they would there obtain a cure. And side by side with these, or trudging past them, came the sturdy fishermen, not daring to venture to sea until they had paid their accustomed visit to the old massive walls, and so "made sure o' guid luck and protection frae danger." There amid the ruins, the first class continued long to pour forth supplications for relief, conveyed in the expressions of a dark and blinding superstition, while the fishermen, contenting themselves with depositing a coin of trifling value on a well-known spot, and uttering one or two hasty ejaculations, hurried away to their perilous duties on the deep.

The ruinous building, formerly the object of so much superstition, is the remains of a chapel, which was dedicated to Tredwell, a Romish saint, who acquired great credit for healing diseases, and for many other pretended miracles. Her chapel became in consequence a celebrated place of resort for the Orcadians, and many a pilgrim knelt before her shrine, and supplicated her assistance and protection. And even when Popery no longer existed in the islands, St. Tredwell still had her devotees who continued during more than two centuries and a half those practices which their forefathers had been taught to believe in as a high and holy devotism; but which, when divested of the adventitious circumstances with which Popery knows so well how to disguise her errors, stood forth in the unadorned garb of the most degrading superstition.

The tradition connected with the superstitious practices which have been described, has been amply verified by the results of an excavation of the ruins of the chapel made some time ago. On removing some of the stones and rubbish at the east end of the chapel, the remains of the altar were discovered. It appears to have been about three feet in width, and projected about two feet from the wall, but its height cannot now be ascertained. On lifting some of the stones there were discovered, in different places, seven copper coins, of the following reigns, viz.,—a copper coin of James VI.; a copper coin marked " Carolus," date effaced ; two half pennies and a farthing of George II. ; one penny and a halfpenny of George III.

If we now cross over to the Holm of Papa Westray we will find a large pictshouse, which was opened by Lieut. Thomas, R.N,, in 1849. Its external appearance is that of an elliptical mound, 115 feet in its largest diameter, and 55 feet in the shorter, and about 10 feet high. It gradually diminishes in height towards the outer side, which formed a facing or wall of about 2 feet in height, circumscribing the building. The entrance on the east side was only 2 feet 8 inches high, and 22 inches wide, and opened into a chamber 45 feet long, and only 5 feet wide at the floor. The walls are perpendicular to the height of 5 feet, but afterwards gradually approximate until at 9 feet from the floor they are within 2 feet 8 inches of each other. There is a chamber at each end of the large apartment, one of them 12 feet long, and the other only 7. There are three entrances on each side of the middle chamber to as many small cells, and in each of the end chambers are also entrances to three cells. Thus the building consists of three central chambers, with twelve smaller cells placed around them—the largest chamber having six cells, and the two end ones three each, averaging between 4 and 5 feet in length, 3 in width, and from 3 to 5½ in length. No organic remains were found in the building.

Lieutenant Thomas thought that he could make out a neatly engraved circle about 4 inches in diameter, on the side wall, near the entrance, and about 6 feet from the floor ; and at a little distance two small circles cut in a stone and touching each other. These

incised figures are in character identical, we believe, with engravings
on the celebrated underground chamber at New Grange, county
Meath, in Ireland;—with those found on a tomb near the great
monument at Carnae, in Brittany, in France;—and with others found
on tombs on an island close to the coast of Brittany.

In 1855, a tomb of a very early class was opened near this pictshouse. It was marked off into three compartments, each about 4
feet long, and about 6 feet wide. Several human skeletons were
found, but all decapitate, except one which lay in the last compartment opened, or rather the skull lay in it—the body stretching away
into another compartment which was left undisturbed. Three skulls
stood side by side immediately in front of the other skull just
mentioned, and others were found throughout the tomb, which also
contained great quantities of animal bones. There were also
carefully spread on a layer of stones a great number of deers' horns,
some very large but much decayed, and portions of the skull
attached to some of them; at least fourteen pairs of horns were
ascertained to have been placed there. The horn cores of the goat
were also found, and this, by the way, is curious, for at the
"Moul" of Papa Westray, there is a well known cave called "*Habra
Helye*," literally the goat's cave.

We may now stay at Papa Westray, or return to Westray, till
the steamer sails for Kirkwall—the usual days being Mondays and
Thursdays. On our return journey, we will visit

Eday.

As we approach this island, we get a magnificent view of the Red
Head, which, when the sun is shining upon it, is of a striking blood
red colour. The steamer touches at Calf Sound, where we land.

The area of the island is fourteen square miles. A large portion
of the island consists of peat, moss, and moorland. Above the landing
place is the residence of the proprietor, H. C. Hebden, Esq.

The little island which lies out in the Sound is known as the Calf of
Eday. It was here John Gow, the original of Cleveland in Sir
Walter Scott's novel of the *Pirate*, was captured. Gow, was a native
of Orkney—his father being a merchant in Stromness. John Gow,

after leaving school, went to sea, and nothing further is known of him till he returned to Orkney in January, 1725. He then commanded an armed ship named the Revenge, of about 200 tons burden, carrying 24 large guns, and six of a smaller size. Gow gave numerous dancing parties, which got him into the good graces of the fair sex; but the insolent and riotous behaviour of his men awakened the suspicions of the people, and plans were formed for the capture of the Revenge and her lawless crew. Thereupon Gow weighed anchor and sailed for Eday, to take vengeance on James Fea of Clestrain, whom he believed to be amongst the most active in planning for his capture. In beating through the entry to Calf Sound on the 13th February, 1725, the Revenge ran aground on the Calf of Eday. The pirate sent a small boat well manned, to Eday for assistance; but James Fea got the men persuaded to go with him to a " change-house " to drink their captain's health, and, with the assistance of some friends, the whole were disarmed and made prisoners.

Some letters afterwards passed between Gow the pirate and Jas. Fea—the pirate also, in his anxiety to get assistance, writing to Mrs Fea, and presenting her with a chintz gown.

At length Gow left his vessel, to speak personally with Fea, when he was made prisoner; and the crew remaining on the vessel were afterwards got off on one pretence or another till the whole were captured, as well as their ship—without one shot having been fired, or a sword drawn.

The fate of captain and crew is soon told. They were tried in the High Court of Admiralty, and Captain Gow, with several of his associates, were condemned, and expiated by an ignominious death, at Execution Dock, London, on the 11th of August, 1729, the crimes which they had so long committed with impunity while lawlessly roving the deep. Often had their ears been shut to the piercing cries for mercy when their victims were compelled to walk the plank which toppled over and plunged them into the foaming ocean, amid the jeers and pitiless taunts of the pirate crew. But now the day of retribution had come, and these merciless rovers were launched into eternity, unpitied by the heartless crowd that witnessed their dying agonies.

We may add that the behaviour of Gow from his first commitment was reserved and morose. He considered himself as an assured victim to the justice of the laws, nor entertained any hope of being admitted on evidence, as Mr Fea had hinted to him he might be. When brought to trial he refused to plead, in consequence of which he was sentenced to be pressed to death in the usual manner. When the officer, however, was about to inflict this punishment, he begged to be taken back to the bar, and having then pleaded " Not Guilty," he was convicted on the same evidence as his accomplices.

Fea is said to have received, from one source and another, £1,800 for the capture of the pirate; but he had to meet a series of prosecutions which were trumped up against him, with the result that he was almost ruined. He afterwards supported Prince Charlie in the rebellion of '45, when a house of his in Shapinsay was burned down by the Hanoverians, whilst Mrs Fea was subjected to very brutal treatment.

On this island where Gow was captured, are two specimens of ancient buildings. One is simply a hole dug in the ground, lined with a rude stone wall, and covered with a large stone slab that is grown over with peat. The interior is of an oval figure, $4\frac{1}{2}$ feet by 3 feet, and about 2 feet high. The entrance is by a low narrow passage at one end, through which a naked savage might contrive to squeeze edgeways and coil himself up in the interior. The entrance was probably concealed by the heather. Not far distant is another of these subterranean buildings displaying somewhat more ingenuity in its construction. An opening about 3 feet high and 2 wide, in the face of a gentle slope, gives admission to this primitive building. On advancing about 5 or 6 feet through the passage, which gradually increases in height, an opening or doorway into a small cell is seen on the right hand. Another opening farther in, on the same side, admits to a somewhat similar but larger cell. On the opposite side is another of the same dimensions, while a fourth runs across the inner ends of the two last mentioned cells. The doorway of the fourth cell is built up, with the exception of a small opening near the roof, through which one might scramble into it. Perhaps the best idea of this building is simply to say that its interior arrangements bear a close resemblance to the forecastle of one of our half-decked fishing boats, having berths on each side, and one across the bow, with scarcely standing room between.

We can now walk along the island, and be at the South End in time to join the steamer when it calls in from Sanday and Stronsay. As we pass along the road we will see a large standing stone, a few pictshouses, and other antiquarian remains.

We also see traces of ancient dykes running across the island, here diving deep beneath the moss, and there again on the hill side cropping above the surface; and one cannot view these without becoming convinced that many long centuries must have elapsed before the peat could have accumulated over these dykes to the depth it is now found to have attained. The race that have left these traces were probably the same people by whom the subterranean dwellings of Saverock, and others of that class, were erected, and to whom the tomb in the holm of Papa Westray belongs.

Having now rejoined the steamer at the South End, a sail of about an hour and a half will bring us back to Kirkwall.

EXCURSION to MAESHOWE, STENNIS, STROMNESS, and HOY.

This, our last excursion, is one of the best to be had in Orkney. Leaving Kirkwall in the morning, we have a pleasant drive along the Ayre, after which we skirt Wideford Hill. As we pass Quanterness we get a delightful view of most of the North Isles, as well as the entire Bay; and shortly afterwards we enter the parish of

Firth.

On the shore of the bay, and not far from the house of Rennibister, stands the well-known tumulus or knoll called Ingashow. The building is only half its original diameter, the side next the shore having been removed, either for supplying stones for neighbouring buildings, or by the encroachments of the sea; probably both these causes have united in the work of destruction.

The wall of the tower is about 14 feet in diameter at the base, the interior or enclosed space about 28 feet, and the total diameter at the base about 56 feet. The part of the wall which was found to remain standing is about 9 feet high. A little above the base on its outer circumference it begins gradually to recede, so that measuring across the top of the ruins it is two feet less in thickness than at the base. In this respect it resembles the bell-shaped tower of Mousa in Shetland, and like it, probably again bulged out at the top; for unquestionably the 9 feet of wall is only a small proportion of the original height of the tower at Ingashow.

The only doorway now to be seen is on the south-west side, and seems to have had outworks for defence opposite its entrance. In general appearance it resembles the doorway of the burg at Burray.

There is a cell in the thickness of the wall on the east side of the main passage. The wall between the cell and the passage is pierced by two or three square holes, through which a spear or other long weapon might have been thrust. About three feet above the floor of the cell there was a stone lintel, apparently belonging to a small passage which had communication with the main passage. At a short distance to the eastward of the cell, the ruins of another of smaller size was discovered, and in it lay fragments of skulls and other portions of human skeletons. Two of them were evidently of very young children. But the skeltons had, in all probability, been placed there after the building had become ruinous. There were indications that there had been another cell in the wall on the west side of the main entrance. The latter was $3\frac{1}{2}$ feet wide at its outer extremity, and continued at that width for 10 feet inwards. At this point, a stone on each side, built perpendicularly in the wall, had its edge projecting a few inches into the passage, and another stone, set on edge, about 6 or 7 inches in height, extending across the passage between the projecting stones. This appeared to have been the remains of the primitive door which was in use when the building was inhabited. That could not have been the golden age, for, " the barring of the door, weel, weel," seems to have been at least as necessary then as now. Immediately outside the stone on edge lay the skeleton of an animal across the passage, the head towards the west side. It was much decomposed and mutilated, but appeared to have been a deer, as pieces of deer's horns were found near the fragments of the skull. Inside the stone which blocked up the doorway the passage was 5 feet 10 inches wide, but again narrowed to its inner extremity, which was only 3 feet 10 inches wide. The height of the passage cannot be ascertained with certainty, as its roof lintels are all wanting, but appearances on the side wall of the passage seem to indicate a height of between 8 and 9 feet. On arriving at the inner extremity of the doorway or main entrance an intruder would still have found a formidable obstacle in his way, for he would only have stepped into a cell or chamber of a triangular figure, whose only communication with the interior of the building was by a diminutive passage about $2\frac{1}{2}$ feet square in the wall on the left hand side of the cell. This wall extended inwards about 10 feet on a line with the west side of the main passage, then made a sharp bend towards the east, and was carried on to a point on the inner circumference of the wall of the tower, about 7 or 8 feet beyond the east side of the doorway. The two sides of the cell formed by the angular wall were made to converge by the overlapping of the successive courses of stones, while, at the same time, they were gradually inclined towards the wall of the tower, until (judging from what is found standing) they united at, and rested on, a point at a considerable height on the inner face of the circular wall. It is difficult to convey a correct idea of the construction of the cell, but if those who have seen the cells in the "pictshouses," were to suppose a cell of that description, say about 10 feet square, to be cut diagonally from top to bottom, and one of the sections to be placed against the inner circumference of the circular wall of the tower, he will then have a tolerable idea of the cell which protected the inner extremity of the doorway of the round tower of Ingashow.

On the removal of the *debris* from the end of the ruins of the circular wall, where it was broken off on the sea beach at the east side, the section showed at the outer circumference a wall about 5 feet 6 inches thick; then, a narrow passage or gallery, 1 foot 9 inches wide, and 6 or 7 feet high, but very dilapidated; next, another wall 3 feet 9 inches thick; and, finally, a third wall, 3 feet thick, thus giving 14 feet as the entire breadth at the base of the circular wall of the tower, including the narrow gallery or passage, which terminated at a point a few feet distant from the east end of the smaller cell in the wall. At this point, also, the several walls composing the main or circular wall, became blended in one solid mass of building, 14 feet thick at the base, and 12 at the top.

Several pieces of deer's horns, fragments of charcoal made from small branches of trees, and animal bones were found among the ruins.

The castle or round tower of Ingashow belongs to the same period in which the castles of Burray, Birsay, and others were built. How ong it existed before the introduction of Christianity into Orkney, who can tell? The skeleton of a deer found within the doorway, as f it had laid itself down there to die, afterthe building had ceased to be nhabited; the charred wood and numerous fragments of deer's horns—all seemed to point to ages long gone by, and to indicate great physical changes in the Orcadian landscape.

In the bay of Firth will be seen the little island of Damsay, upon which, like the island of Enhallow, neither rats nor mice can exist—at least tradition says so. Swein Asliefson, after murdering Swein Brióstreip at Orphir, took shelter in a castle on this little island. It was on this same island that Earls Rognvald and Harald surprised Earl Erlend. The latter Earl, with his men, were in the Castle here, drinking all day, and at night were surprised by Rognvald and Harald. According to the *Saga*, Erlend was "dead drunk," when attacked, and after the battle was over his body was found under a heap of sea-weed, with a spear through it.

We now drive up to the pretty little village of

Finstown,

Which is quite a thriving place, with its three churches—Established, Free, and U.P.—its bakery, and postal and telegraph office. This is considered half way to Stromness, and a short stay is generally made to refresh the horses.

As we leave the village the mansion-house of Binscarth is seen on the hill on the right, whilst down in the valley there is a nice little glen. A little further along, the road for Harray, Birsay, and Sandwick branches off to the right, and on the left, before us, we have a good view of the battle-field of Summerdale, to which we alluded in our description of Orphir. We also get glimpses of the Loch of Stennis, with the famous Standing Stones. After a few minutes' drive, we see on our right

Maeshowe

Itself, which is conical-shaped, and rises like a little hill on the surrounding plain. If we cross over to Tormiston, the farm on the other side of the road, we will get a guide to take us through the tumulus, as also a light to enable us to see the Runic characters

and ornamentations.   Maeshowe was opened by Mr Farrer, M.P.,
in the summer of 1861.   This conical tumulus is about 92 feet
in diameter and 36 feet high, and is surrounded, at a distance
of 86 feet from the base, by a trench about 20 feet wide, and 4 or 5
feet deep.   The passage is two feet four inches wide at its mouth,
and appears to have been the same in height, but the covering stones
had been removed for about 22½ feet.   It then increases in dimensions
to 3¼ feet in width, and 4 feet 4 inches in height, and continues so
for 26 feet, when it is again narrowed by two upright stone slabs to
2 feet 5 inches.   These slabs are each 2 feet 4 inches broad, and
immediately beyond them the passage extends 2 feet 10 inches, and
then opens into the central chamber.   Its dimensions from the slabs
to its opening into the chamber are 3 feet 4 inches wide, and 4 feet
8 inches high.   About 34 feet from the outer extremity of the
passage, and about 15 inches beyond the point where its dimensions
are increased to 3¼ feet in width and 4 feet 4 inches in height, there
is a triangular recess in the wall, about 2 feet deep and 8½ feet in
height and width in front, and there was found lying opposite to it
in the passage a large block of stone of corresponding figure and
dimensions.   This block suggests the idea that it had been used to
shut up the passage at the point where it begins to be narrower
towards its outer extremity, and that it was pushed back into the
recess in the wall when admission into the chamber was desired.
From the recess to the chamber the sides of the passage are formed
by immense slabs of flagstone.   One on the north side is upwards of
19 ft. long and 4½ in. thick.   The floor is also paved with flagstones.

On emerging from the passage we enter a chamber about 15 feet
square on the level of the floor, and about 13 feet in height to the
top of the present walls.   Immediately in front opposite to the
passage is an opening in the wall 3 feet from the floor.   This is the
entrance to a cell or small chamber in the wall, 5 feet 8½ inches long,
four and a half feet wide, and three and a half feet high.   A large
flagstone is laid as a raised floor between the entrance and the inner
end of the chamber.   The entrance passage is two feet wide, two and
a half feet high, and twenty-two and a half inches long.

On the two opposite walls of the chamber, to the right and left are similar openings nearly on a similar level with that just described. The opening on the right is two feet and a half wide, two feet nine and a half inches high, one foot eight inches long, and two feet eight inches above the floor of the chamber. The cell to which it gives admission is six feet ten inches long, four feet seven inches wide, three and a half feet high, and has a raised flagstone floor, five and a half inches high, similar to the other chamber. The opening on the left is two and a quarter feet wide, two and a half feet high, and one and three-quarters feet long, and about three feet above the floor of the chamber. The cell, which is entered through this opening, is five feet seven inches long, four feet eight inches wide, and three feet four inches high. It has no raised floor like the two other cells. The roofs, floors, and back walls of the cells are each formed by a single slab of stone, and blocks of stone, corresponding in size and figure to the openings, were found on the floor in front of them. These have been to close the entrances of the cells. The four walls of the chamber converge towards the top by the successive projection of each course of the masonry, commencing about six feet above the level of the floor, in a manner exactly similar to the construction of the so-called pictshouses of Quanterness and Wideford Hill. By this means the chamber would be brought to a narrow space of probably a few feet square at top, and then completed by slabs laid across the opening horizontally or on edge. The upper portion, however, has been removed at some former period, and the highest part of the walls is now only about 13 feet from the floor. At that point the opposite walls have approached to within 10 feet of each other, so that the ruins of the chamber are now 15 feet square, at the floor, and about 10 feet square at the top of the walls, as they now stand. Its original height has been probably 19 or 20 feet, and the clay has then been piled above the roof to a height of several feet.

A large buttress stands in each angle of the chamber to strengthen the walls and support them under the pressure of their own weight, and of the superincumbent clay. These internal buttresses vary somewhat in dimensions, but they are on an average about 3 feet square at the base, and are from 9 to 10 feet high, with the exception of one, which is now only 8 feet high, and one of the sides of each buttress is formed by a single slab.

The most interesting circumstance connected with the explorations was the discovery of 700 or 800 Runic characters on the walls and buttresses of the chambers, and on the walls of the cells. They were in general very perfect, and only in one or two instances did they appear to have become illegible. The figure of a dragon is beautifully cut on one of the buttresses, and displays great spirit and artistic skill. Beneath it are other figures, one of which has a resemblance to a serpent twined around a tree or pole.

The walls of the chamber are built with large slabs, which generally extend the entire length of the wall, and the whole building displays great strength and skill in the masonry, and has a very imposing effect.

There is every reason to believe that the building was originally erected as a chambered tomb for some chief or person of great note, and probably long before the arrival of the Norsemen in Orkney. That it has, however, been entered by them is proved by the Runes, but that it was very likely becoming ruinous when they found it, appears from evidences on the stones of their perishing condition when the Runes were cut on them.

Professor Blackie visited Maeshowe in 1868, and he says that he was led " through a passage long and low, with mighty massonrie,"

. . . . " And soon beneath
  A chambered vault we stood
Of shapely stones with chilly glance
  Of earthy drip bedewed.

And where the glimmering torch was held—
  The tale I tell is true—
A dragon shape upon the wall
  Uncouthly came to view—

A dragon of the scaly brood,
  Like dire Chimera old,
Transfixed upon the bristling back
  By lance of hero bold.

A dragon dire, and eke a snake—
  A snake, whose glittering twine
Embraced a rod, like Hermes' wand,
  I saw with wondering eyne.

> And right and left the dripping wall
>   Was lettered strangely round
> With sculpture rude, to tell the tale
>   Of him who built the mound.
>
> But what it told of saga old
>   And stout sea-roaving loons,
> I might not know : much wiser men
>   May spell the mystic Runes.
>
> This only lore my beggar wit
>   Could easily understand,
> That mighty men had lived of yore,
>   And died in Orkney land."

With regard to the Runic characters already referred to, they were submitted to Professors Stephens, Munch, Rafn, and Barclay, for translation. Though much information was expected, little was got. Large numbers of the Runes gave the names of those who carved them, whilst others hinted at some wealth which was buried in the vicinity; but the Professors, almost in no case, gave the same rendering of any passage. One of the inscriptions regarding a lady is thus translated by Professor Stephens—" *Ingibiorgh, the fair lady. Many a woman hath fared Skin-clad (or bent) here, (who) great wealth owned.*" Professor Munch's reading of the same passage is— " *Ingiburg, the fair widow! Many a woman has wandered stooping in here (although) ever so haughty.*" Professor Rafn translates the same passage thus—" *Ingiborg, the fair widow, or Ingiborg the fair, the widow. Many a rather proud woman did walk here stooping (bent forward), or did walk stooping here in (into).* Annexed we give a specimen of the Rune characters found in Maeshowe.

Professor Rafn, writing to the *Orcadian* newspaper of September 14, 1861, though he gave no indication of the probable age of the mound, pointed out that the reference to Ingibiorg was an evidence of itself that the inscription belonged to the eleventh or twelfth

I

century. Principal Barclay, however, hazards the opinion that the mound was raised at the latter part of the eighth, or beginning of the ninth, century.

We now take a walk of about ten minutes along the public road towards Stromness, till we come to the branch road on our right, which strikes up towards the Established Church, and in a few minutes we are in the vicinity of

The Standing Stones of Stennis.

"Those huge old stones so grey with age,
Have they no place in history's page—
No record of the past to tell
Of bloody rites, or mystic spell,
Of victims at the altar bound
On yonder stone-encircled ground.

We come, we wonder, and we gaze
On those remains of other days :
But none can lift the close dark veil,
Or read their old and wondrous tale.
Perhaps within that stony ring
The Judges held the ancient "Ting "*
Where Justice swift and stern was given,
Beneath the canopy of Heaven :
And near at hand the temple stood
Where priestly hands were dipp'd in blood,
Ah ! if those hoary blocks could speak,
Their words might blanch the ruddiest cheek,
And make the stoutest heart to quail
At many a dark and ghastly tale.
Methinks I see the victim's face
Paled by the horrors of the place ;
Methinks I hear his fearful cry
Pierce upwards to the vaulted sky.
No pity moves the circling throng,
As through the midst he's dragg'd along,
No friendly eye is dimm'd with tears,
No kindly voice allays his fears ;
But all around the savage cries
Too surely tell the victim dies.
'Twere fitting that such scenes of blood
Should be where tongueless records stood ;
So close by yonder water's side
Should flow the fearful crimson tide—
That in the lake's oblivious wave
The victim's blood might find a grave ;
And when in future ages man
Should seek those bygone rites to scan,
And know the circle's history,
Those huge old stones should silent be."

* "Ting " or "Thing," the ancient Scandinavian Court of Justice.

The object and time of erection of these stones are involved in mystery. They were undoubtedly standing there at the time of the Scandinavian invasion, for in the oldest Sagas the promontory on which they stand is called " *Steinsness,*" thereby proving that their remarkable appearance suggested the name to the Norwegian invaders. And there is no evidence to show that they may not have stood there in all their rude grandeur when the Celtic race supplanted a still earlier population.

THE STANDING STONES OF STENNIS.

The Standing Stones of Stennis are in several groups, of which the most remarkable are those termed the Circle of Stennis, and the Ring of Brogar. The former of these is on the south side of the Bridge of Brogar, near the edge of the Loch of Stennis, and at a short distance from the public road. A great portion of the circle is destroyed, but it appears to have been about 235 feet in diameter, measuring from the outer edge of the embankment. The original number of the stones composing the Circle was probably 12, although only two now remain standing, the tallest of which is 18 feet in height, 4 feet 7 inches in breadth at the base, much broader at the top, and about 11 inches thick. The other stone is $15\frac{3}{4}$ feet high, and much thicker and broader than its neighbour. Another very large block of stone, 18 feet long, and calculated to weigh upwards of ten tons, lies on the ground, having been thrown down in 1815. The circle, when complete, must have had a very imposing appearance. The remains of a cromlech are still visible within the circle. It is not in the centre, but towards one side, and the remains of the flat top stone still rest partially on two of the upright stones which have been pushed latterly outwards from beneath it. The perforated stone of Odin stood to the northward, near the Bridge of Brogar, and at the south end of the bridge the immense " Watch Stone " raises its hoary head. The hole that was cut through the upper part of this Stone of Odin was for the purpose, it is supposed, of tying the sacrificial victim ; but in after years it was used in quite another way. When young people fell in love, they resorted to the Stone of Odin, and, joining hands through it, plighted their troths. " When the parties had agreed to marry, they repaired to the temple of the Moon, where the woman, in presence of the man, fell down on her knees and prayed to the God Woden (for such was the name of the god whom they addressed on this occasion) that he would enable her to perform all the promises and obligations she had made, and was to make, to the young man present ; after which they both went to the temple of the Sun, where the man prayed in like manner before the woman. Then they went to the Stone of Odin ; and the man being on the one side, and the woman on the other, they took hold of each other's right hand through the hole in it, and there swore to be constant and faithful to each other." When the couple wished to annul this vow, they simply repaired to the Church of Stennis—the one passing out at the north door, the other at the south—and the thing was done. It is said that the people used to leave offerings at the stone ; and there was a prevalent belief to the effect that a child who was passed through the Stone of Odin would never shake with the palsy. The large circle of Standing Stones is on a slope on the north side of the bridge, and is 366 feet in diameter, measuring from the inner edge of the ditch which surrounds the circle of stones. The ditch or trench is about 29 feet wide, 6 feet of average depth, and inclose a space containing nearly 2½ acres. The number of stones in this ring was probably 60 originally, but 13 are now only standing, and 10 are lying on the ground, besides several stumps. The highest stone standing is 13 feet 3 inches, and the lowest 4½ feet; but the latter has evidently been broken. The ground within the circle has never been levelled.

On the top of a low hill, a little way beyond the half circle, there is a very extensive ancient quarry from which there is good reason to believe that many of the Standing Stones have been taken. Proceeding a short distance further along the crest of the hill the Ridge of Bookan is reached. It is a circular space surrounded by a deep trench sharply defined. There are no traces of standing stones around the circumference of this circle, but stumps of small stones and large blocks are still visible near its centre. The internal area of the Ring is 136 feet, the breadth of trench 44 feet, and its depth about 6 feet.

There are large earth mounds in the neighbourhood of the Circles. In one near the large circles a very large stone cinerary urn was found a few years ago, and in another a flint spear-head, and fragments of small vessels or urns of burnt clay with human skeletons, the whole furnishing proof of great antiquity for these aboriginal remains.

Excellent trout fishing may be had on the Loch of Stennis, especially at the bridges of Waith and Brogar.

Taking our seats in our conveyance, we now drive westwards, through Stennis, and in little over half-an-hour, upon reaching the summit of the hill near where the Sandwick Road joins the Kirkwall and Stromness Road, we have a very pretty view of Stromness and its romantic surroundings. Below us lies by far the best harbour in the county, being large and splendidly sheltered by the island of Græmsay, the Ness, and the Holms. The town itself is seen nestling on the slopes of Brinkie's Braes, whilst beyond tower the sombre hills of Hoy, guarding this favoured little place from the wild blasts of the Atlantic. "Southwards the sea is studded with the islands of Cava, Phara, and Flotta, which intercept the view in this direction. In the quiet of an autumn night, when the sky is red above the northern sea, one feels the presence of another world around him—the presence of a deep tranquility embosomed in a circle of rounded islets,—and as the glare of the aurora borealis dies away, the dream of peace seems vanished too." In a couple of minutes more, we are traversing the streets of

Stromness.

The parishes of Stromness and Sandwick form the west and south-west boundary of the Mainland, and contain about 31 square miles. The town of Stromness, at the beginning of last century, had scarcely any existence, and consisted of a few fishermen's huts. Possessing good natural advantages, however, it continued to grow; the population in 1881 was 2410. Until about forty years ago, Stromness harbour was a great resort for vessels of all nations. At one time as many as 800 entered the harbour yearly. It was frequented by whaling vessels, that shipped a considerable portion of their crews here. The harbour is sheltered on the east by two holms, on the south by the island of Græmsay, and on the west by the hills of Hoy. Its entrance, which is from the south, is about a quarter of a mile broad, and it extends to a mile in length. There is an excellent roadstead outside the harbour, which can afford equally safe and much more commodious anchorage. The town is irregular in construction, but is exceedingly healthy, and possesses good hotel accommodation. There is a wharf for the accommodation of vessels, and a great number of quays attached to dwelling houses, for the convenience of small boats. There are three churches in town—Established, Free, and U.P. Lead abounds in the neighbourhood; there are also mineral springs. The geological formation of the district is very interesting. The island of Græmsay, extending about a mile and a half from east to west, is about the same distance from Stromness, and has a light-house at each end. The steamer St Olaf leaves Stromness for Scapa and Thurso, carrying the mails, daily, and there is bi-weekly communication to and from the south—by the North of Scotland and Orkney and Shetland Steam Navigation Company's steamers, and the steamers of the Messrs Langlands. Though Stromness, compared with Kirkwall, may be said to be in its infancy, it has a history not devoid of interest. In the days when Jo Ben visited it, though then a mere hamlet, it must have witnessed many stirring scenes, as French and Spanish vessels were in the habit of resorting to it for shelter. Then when the whalers called here to get their crews completed, the hamlet increased to a town, and the frequent visits made by the Hudson Bay Company's vessels added to its prosperity.

In the year 1754, the people of Stromness complained of the " vexatious, unrelenting and illegal severity " of the assessments laid

STROMNESS.

upon them by the Royal Burgh of Kirkwall, and refused to submit to such treatment any longer. The matter was then taken before the Court of Session—decision being pronounced against Kirkwall. An appeal was taken to the House of Lords, and in 1758, a final decision was given in favour of Stromness. This plucky action on the part of Stromness freed all other places in Scotland similarly situated, from the illegal assessments which the royal burghs had hitherto enforced.

Stromness is also famous as having given subjects to the poet and to the novelist. George Stewart, son of Mr Stewart of Mussater, is the "Torquil" of Lord Byron's poem "The Island." That unfortunate young man spent his younger days at the White House, Stromness. He was a midshipman on the "Bounty," and though he was not one of the mutineers, he was placed in irons on the "Pandora," and was lost in that vessel when returning to England. This, and the death of his Otaheitan wife of a broken heart, awakened the muse of Byron, who says :—

> "And who is he ; the blue-eyed northern child
> Of isles more known to man, but scarce less wild ;
> The fair-haired offspring of the Hebrides,
> Where roars the Pentland with its whirling seas ;
> Rock'd in his cradle by the roaring wind,
> The tempest-born in body and in mind,
> His young eyes opening on the ocean foam,
> Had from that moment deem'd the deep his home,
> The giant comrade of his pensive moods,
> The sharer of his craggy solitudes,
> The only mentor of his youth, where'er
> His bark was born ; the sport of wave and air ;
> A careless thing, who placed his choice in chance,
> Nursed by the legends of his land's romance,
> Eager to hope, but not less firm to bear,
> Acquainted with all feelings save despair."

Sir Walter Scott also got the chief characters for his novel the *Pirate*, at Stromness. Gow, or as Scott calls him, Cleveland, whose capture we described at pages 111 and 112, was born in a house on Cairston shore, and spent his school-boy days at Stromness. When in 1725, he visited his native town, with his pirate ship the "Revenge," he is said to have fallen in love with a Miss Gordon, and, according to tradition, they pledged their troth to each other at the Stone of Odin, as described at page 124. After Gow's execution in 1729, Miss Gordon travelled all the way to London, where she touched the hand of her dead lover, that she might be released from the vow she had made at the Stone of Odin. Bessie Miller, the prototype of "Norna of the Fitful Head," lived in Stromness, and died at the ripe old age of nearly 100 years. Scott says she "helped out her subsistence by selling favourable winds to mariners. He was a venturous master of a vessel who left the roadstead of Stromness without paying his offering to propitiate Bessie Miller ; her fee was extremely moderate, being exactly sixpence, for which, as she explained herself, she boiled her kettle and gave the bark advantage of her prayers, for she disclaimed all unlawful arts. The wind thus petitioned for was sure, she said, to arrive, though sometimes the mariners had to wait some time for it. The woman's dwelling and appearance were not unbecoming her pretensions; her house, which was on the brow of the steep hill on which Stromness is founded, was only accessible by a series of dirty and precipitous lanes, and for exposure might have been the abode of Æolus himself, in whose commodities the inhabitant dealt. She herself was, as she told us, nearly one hundred years old, withered and dried up like a mummy. A clay coloured kerchief, folded round her head, corresponded in colour to her corpse-like complexion. Two light blue eyes that gleamed with a lustre like that of insanity, an utterance of astonishing rapidity, a nose and chin that almost met together, and a ghastly expression of cunning, gave her the effect of Hecaté. She remembered Gow the pirate, who had been a native of these islands in which he closed his career. Such was Bessie Miller, to whom the mariners paid a sort of tribute." Mammie Scott succeeded Bessie Miller, in the sale of favourable winds, and "many wonderful tales are told of her power and influence over the weather. . . . . A captain called upon Mammie one day to solicit a fair wind. He was bound for Stornoway, and received from the reputed witch a scarlet thread upon which were three knots. His instructions were that if sufficient wind did not arrive one of the knots was to be untied; if that proved insufficient, another knot was to be untied; but he was on no account to unloose the third knot, else disaster would overtake his vessel. The mariner set out upon his voyage, and, the wind being light, untied the first knot. This brought a stronger breeze, but still not sufficient to satisfy him. The second knot was let down, and away the vessel sped across the waters round Cape Wrath. In a short time the entrance to Stornoway harbour was reached, when it came into the Captain's head to untie the third knot in order to see what might occur. He was too near the end of his voyage to suffer any damage now, and so he felt emboldened to make the experiment. No sooner was the last knot set free than a perfect hurricane set in

from a contrary direction, which drove the vessel right back to Hoy
Sound, from which he had set out, where he had ample time to repent
of his folly.   On another occasion the skipper of a schooner happened
to shoot some of Mammie's ducks, for which offence he was severely
punished.   His vessel was driven upon a shoal of rock, and was with
much difficulty got off.   He went and apologised to Mammie Scott,
but it was a long time ere he pacified the old crone, who, having
received some money, finally permitted him to get a fair wind, adding,
however, that he must not shoot any more of her ducks.

" An old sea captain informed the writer that, on one occasion in
his young days, he was relieved of the sum of 15s by some one in
Stromness.   He went to Mammie and consulted her about his loss.
She informed him that his money had been taken by a person closely
connected with himself, and, if he made a great fuss about the matter,
he would find the money returned that night, and concealed under
his pillow.   It happened as she had predicted: the cash was found
amongst the straw beneath his bolster !   One plan of Mammie's
for bringing fair winds was that of cutting a pack of cards in different
ways.   But wind was not the only commodity in which she trafficked.
She had the reputation of depriving people of their senses, in fact, of
driving them mad. A certain man's wife was rendered insane through
Mammie's influence, it was said, and the plan adopted by her husband
to restore her to a sound mind was both original and remarkable.
He tied a rope round the woman, and towed her behind his boat up
and down the harbour.   But it had no effect; she bobbed about
behind the boat like a cork, and remained as mad as ever.   The
remarkable thing is that she wasn't drowned.   A young woman in
one of the South Isles was also rendered insane, through the evil
influence of the Stromness witch, and did not regain her reason until
her sweetheart had propitiated Mammie.   People considered it a just
punishment when her own daughter went out of her mind and
remained insane all her life."

Passing along to the south end of the town, we come to the Town
Hall, which was built by public subscription.   Above the Hall there
is a Museum, which, though not well kept, is worth a visit, as

there are many curiosities in it. The first place, of course, is given to Orcadian fossils, and the most attractive of these is the Asterolepis, which was found by Hugh Miller at the Black Crag. It is not quite six inches in length; yet it is part of a monster fish which varies in length from 8 to 23 feet.

Leaving the Museum, and proceeding southwards, we soon reach Breckness, where "part of a Burg remains in the face of a cliff, the rest having been carried away by the action of the sea. The curvature of the remaining wall shows that this Burg has been originally a circle of 44 feet, inner diameter, and the thickness of the wall is 12 feet, so that the outer diameter has been 68 feet. Of this about 15 feet only remain, and upwards of 50 feet have been carried away. Now, the Burg stands on solid sandstone rock, and it is apparent that before 50 feet of the rock were wasted away here, the point of Breckness must have extended at least 50 feet farther out, and probably more. The *minimum* time, therefore, that can have elapsed since the building of this Burg must be sufficient to allow for the wasting away of 50 feet of a shore line consisting of solid sandstone cliffs of the height of 30 or 40 feet, in a locality where no perceptible change has taken place in the memory of the existing generation. Those who know the slow rate at which a solid rocky coast is wasted away must feel that such facts as are exhibited by the section of the Burg cliff at Breckness are altogether incompatible with any theory that assigns the origin of Burgs to a recent period. This instance is not a solitary one, for in many other cases, and even in sheltered situations and on inland lakes, a large part of the circle of Orcadian Burgs has been carried away by the wasting of the coast line, but the section exposed at Breckness is so striking that it is unnecessary to refer to others."

Here, also, is Breckness House, the remains of an old mansion which was erected by Bishop Græme. In the same locality may be seen the ruins of the old Church of Stromness, surrounded by a graveyard, as well as the remains of an ancient monastery.

The next place of interest is the Black Crag, which is over 360 feet in height. During a terrific gale of south-west wind on

Wednesday, 5th March, 1834, the schooner Star of Dundee was wrecked here, in presence of hundreds of spectators, who could do nothing to aid the unfortunate crew. When the vessel struck, every soul on board was supposed to be lost. On the Sunday following, however, one of the crew made his appearance, who had been saved in the most miraculous way. He was driven into the only cave to be found in the ridge of rocks, which is now known as Charlie's Hole. During the time he was imprisoned in the cave, he fed upon red herrings, a barrel of which had been providentially cast in beside him. His thirst he quenched by catching, in a tin oil can, the water which dripped from the rocks.

Under the Black Crag is the old red sandstone fossil-bed where Hugh Miller discovered the Asterolepis, and where he gathered the chief materials for the " Footprints of the Creator, or, the Asterolepis of Stromness."

A walk of about a quarter of an hour, along one of the prettiest coast lines in Orkney, will bring us to North Gaulton Castle. This huge rock has been separated from the adjoining headland by the action of the Atlantic, and, at a distance, somewhat resembles the Old Man of Hoy.

Retracing our steps to Stromness, we can hire a boat for about 10s to take us across the Sound which separates Hoy from the Mainland.

If wind and tide are favourable, the sail is an enjoyable one, of about one hour's duration. After leaving Stromness Harbour, we sail close past the island of Græmsay, then past the Glen which separates the Ward and Cuilag's Hills, past the Geo of Selwick, and Selwick Little, and then we land at Linksness, on the island of

Hoy,

Which is the prettiest island of the group, with its wild mountain scenery, and its secluded, romantic valleys. Here, too, we shall

"See Hoy's Old Man! whose summit bare,
Pierces the dark blue fields of air ;
Based in the sea, his fearful form
Glooms like the spirit of the storm ;
An Ocean Babel, rent and worn

By time and tide—all wild and lorn ;
A giant that had warred with heaven,
Whose ruined scalp seems thunder-riven ;
Whose form the misty spray doth shroud,
Whose head the dark and hovering cloud—
Around his dread and lowering mass,
In sailing swarms, the sea-fowl pass.
But when the night-cloud o'er the sea
Hangs like a sable canopy,
And when the flying storm doth scourge,
Around his base the rushing surge,
Swift to his airy cliffs they soar
And sleep amid the tempest's roar ;
Or with its howling round his peak,
Mingle their drear and dreamy shriek."

Near the Old Man of Hoy (which will be more fully described further on), at the Stower, the Albion of Blyth was lost in November, 1815. Peterkin, in describing the wreck, mentions that all hands but two had been washed overboard before the vessel struck the rock. One of the survivors was lying insensible on the deck, whilst the other was lashed to the rigging. Some Rackwick fishermen visited the wreck, and, after purloining the cargo, seized the sailor who was lying on the deck, carried him to a shelf of the rock, and left him there " all night—a night of November, when the earth was buried in deep snow, when an intense frost prevailed, and when a piercing sea wind would have chilled to death, on the rocks of Hoy, the most vigorous human being, if exposed in a state of inaction to its power." The poor man was found dead next day, as was his unfortunate comrade, who had been left tied to the rigging. In connection with this incident there is a tradition that the Rev. Gavin Hamilton, who was then minister of Hoy, had in a dream witnessed the whole affair, and astonished the inhuman wreckers by taxing them with their crime, which they thought was known only to themselves.

The Hoy people are credited with being plain and outspoken, and, if the following anecdote can be relied upon, the description is certainly not inappropriate :—" A Hoy ' Hawk' went to his minister, and said, 'Oh! sir, but the ways of Providence are wonderful! I thocht I had met with a sair misfortune, when I lost baith my coo and my wife at aince over the cliff, twa months' sin ; but I gaed ower to Graimsay, and I hae gotten a far better coo and a far bonnier wife."

At one time Hoy was a favourite haunt of eagles, but now they are rarely, if ever, seen there. Writing in 1815, however, Sir Walter Scott says "the clergyman of Hoy told his party that a man had been lately alive, who, when an infant, had been transported from a neighbouring island by an eagle, and carried over a broad sound or arm of the sea, to the bird's nest in Hoy. Pursuit being instantly made, and the eagle's nest being known, the infant was found there, playing with the young eaglets. A more ludicrous instance of transportation the minister himself witnessed. Walking in the fields he heard the squeaking of a pig for some time without being able to discover whence it proceeded, until, looking up, he beheld the unfortunate grunter in the talons of an eagle, who soared away with him to the summit of Hoy."

Leaving Linksness, we strike to the left, and a walk of over half-an-hour, takes us to the far-famed Dwarfie Stone, which Sir

THE DWARFIE STONE.

Walter Scott has immortalised in the *Pirate*. Norna is described as visiting this lonely place, for the purpose of using incantations " to raise the spirit of the vanished Trolld, the elfin dwarf." " It happened on a hot summer day, and just about the hour of noon," says Norna,

" as I sat by the Dwarfie Stone, with my eyes fixed on the Ward-hill, whence the mysterious and ever-burning carbuncle shed its rays more brightly than usual, and repining in my heart at the restricted bounds of human knowledge, that at length I could not help exclaiming, in the words of an ancient Saga,

> ' Dwellers of the mountain, rise,
> Trolld the powerful, Haims the wise !
> Ye who taught weak woman's tongue
> Words that sway the wise and strong,—
> Ye who taught weak woman's hand
> How to wield the magic wand,
> And wake the gales on Foulah's steep
> Or lull wild Sumburgh's waves to sleep !—
> Still are ye yet ?—Not yours the power
> Ye knew in Odin's mightier hour.
> What are ye now but empty names,
> Powerful Trolld, sagacious Haims,
> That lightly spoken, lightly heard,
> Float on the air like thistle's beard ?' "

After the utterance of these words the bright summer day suddenly changed, the sky became overcast with thunder clouds, and the pelting rain fell heavily, inducing Norna to seek the welcome shelter of the Dwarfie Stone. While seated there her active mind began to conjecture concerning the origin of the place. " Had it been really the work of that powerful Trolld, to whom the poetry of the scalds referred it ? Or was it the tomb of some Scandinavian chief, interred with his arms and his wealth, perhaps also with his immolated wife, that what he loved best in life might not in death be divided from him ? Or was it the abode of penance, chosen by some devoted anchorite of later days? Or the idle work of some wandering mechanic, whom chance, and whim, and leisure, had thrust upon such an undertaking ?" Sir Walter, in a note upon this stone, says, "the Orcadian traditions allege the work to be that of a dwarf, to whom they ascribe supernatural powers, and a malevolent disposition, the attributes of that race in Norse mythology. Whoever inhabited this singular den certainly enjoyed

> ' Pillows cold, and sheets not warm.'

I observed that, commencing just opposite to the Dwarfie Stone, and extending in a line to the sea-beach, there are a number of barrows, or cairns, which seem to connect the stone with a very large cairn where we landed. This curious monument may therefore have been intended as a temple of some kind to the Northern *Dii Manes*, to which the cairns might direct worshippers."

From the foregoing it will be seen that Scott has taken hold of a tradition, that a dwarf and his wife made the place their abode; but on the other hand Jo Ben informs us that in his day the myth was that it was the residence of a giant and his wife. The stone is nearly 32 feet long, and about half as broad. There are something like three small apartments hollowed out in it, and in one of which there is a small space 5 feet 2 inches long, and 2 feet broad, that is supposed to be a bed. Wallace says the stone has been " hollowed by the hand of some mason (for the prints of the iron are to be seen on it to this day), with a square hole of about 2 feet high for the entry, and a stone proportional standing before it for a door. Within, at one end, is a bed, excellently cut out of the stone, with a pillow, wherein two men may lie together their full length; at the other end is a couch, and in the middle a hearth for a fire, with a round hole cut out for a chimney. It stands in a desolate, melancholy place, more than a mile from any inhabited house, and all the ground above it is nothing but high heath and heather. It is thought to have been the residence of some melancholy hermit."

In the sleeping apartment are several names which have been cut out by visitors. One runs " H. Ross, 1735," being the name of a gentleman, a native of Perthshire, who settled near Longhope some time last century, descendants of whom still reside there. Close beside it is another, " P. Folster, 1830 "; and beneath, " H. Miller, 1846." Hugh Miller mentions the cutting of his name within this famous stone in the *Cruise of the Betsy*, thus :—" The rain still pattered heavily overhead, and with my geological hammer I did, to beguile the time, what I very rarely do—added my name to the others, in characters which, if both they and the Dwarfie Stone get but fairplay, will be distinctly legible two centuries hence." " Upon the outside of the stone a Persian gentleman, Guilemus Mounsey, has written his name in large capital letters, from right to left, with the date A.D. 1850. Some

Persian poetry is inscribed underneath in the native characters. This gentleman, who was of a rather eccentric turn, slept a night or two within the Dwarfie Stone, and, with his Persian slippers and long flowing robe, astonished the peaceful inhabitants of Hoy, who imagined they again saw the long vanished Dwarf, returned to claim his own."

Above the Dwarfie Stone are the Craw Hamars, massive cliffs of sandstone, from which the Dwarfie Stone itself is supposed to have fallen. On the face of the Ward Hill above us, the carbuncle, to which Norna referred in her musings at the Dwarfie Stone, was at one time to be seen ; but the inhabitants of Hoy now treat it as a myth. Wallace, however, says of it, "that in the months of May, June, and July, about mid-day, is seen something that shines and sparkles admirably, and which is often seen a great way off. It hath shined more brightly before than it does now; tho' many have climbed up the hill and attempted to search for it, yet they could find nothing. The vulgar talk of it as some enchanted carbuncle; but I take it to be some water sliding down the face of a smooth rock, which, when the sun at such a time shines upon it, the reflection causeth the admirable splendour."

We retrace our steps towards Linksness, and pass round the northern slopes of the Cuilags Hill, till we reach the Meadow of the Kame, a crescent-shaped valley, where there is a fine echo. We ascend the Kame from this point, and will have to take advantage of the heather to pull ourselves up. From the summit of the Kame we have about an hour's walk along a magnificent coast-line, of wildest grandeur, at the foot of which, far below us, rolls the ever-restless Atlantic.

The coast line is now reached, where

> "The old man of Hoy
> Looks out on the sea,
> Where the tide runs strong and the wave rides free :
> He looks on the broad Atlantic sea,
> And the old man of Hoy
> Hath this great joy,
> To think on the pride of the sea-kings old,
> Harrolds, and Ronalds, and Sigurds bold,
> Whose might was felt
> By the cowering Celt,

K

When he heard their war-cry yelling;
       But the sea-kings are gone,
       And he stands alone,
Firm on his old rock-dwelling,
       This stout old man of Hoy.

       " But listen to me
       Old man of the sea,
List to the Skulda that speaketh by me;
The Nornies are weaving a web for thee,
       Thou old man of Hoy,
       To ruin thy joy,
And to make thee shrink from the lash of the ocean,
And teach thee to quake with a strange commotion,
       When over thy head
       And under thy bed,
The rampart wave is swelling,
       And thou shalt die
       'Neath a pitiless sky,
And reel from thine old rock-dwelling,
       Thou stout old man of Hoy !''

The Old Man could at one time boast of two legs; but they were so incessantly pounded by the Atlantic that one of them gave way, and the other must soon follow suit, when the old fellow will doubtless make his first and last bow, and then retire from the scene.

THE OLD MAN OF HOY.

On our way towards Rackwick, we pass on the right Rora Head, over which we see Dunnet Head, Scrabster, and Thurso.

From Rackwick, the view of the cliff line towards The Berry, is very imposing. When we join the public road, we make straight for Linksness. On our left is the burn of Berridale, which noisily rushes over the cliffs like a miniature river. Steep cliffs rise on each side of the valley, whilst the little birch trees are richly circled with honeysuckle, which in the summer months load the air with a sweet fragrance that may be felt long before the fairy spot comes in sight. A little beyond this we pass Red Glen on the right, and Sandy Loch on the left, and just as we approach our starting point, we see the Manse, also on the left, which is nicely surrounded with a hedge of fuchsias.

We may now proceed to the southern end of the island, in which is situated the parish of

Walls.

This parish, as well as the parish of Hoy, is the sole property of J. G. Moodie-Heddle, Esq., of Melsetter. The parish of Walls is fertile, and a good grazing district. It contains many objects of antiquarian interest, several brochs, and many tumuli in various parts of the island, which, though worthy of exploration, have yet remained undisturbed. It possesses one of the finest and most picturesque bays in Orkney, and if accommodation on a more extensive scale were provided—it presently has but one inn with good accommodation—and communication with the mainland more frequent, it would be a favourite resort of tourists, for whilst its bays are well adapted for bathing, they also contain the various fish native to Orkney, where the angler could indulge his piscatorial proclivities to an unlimited extent without hindrance. The sportsman might also secure many of the birds fast becoming extinct in the Orkneys. The parish of Walls also possesses two inland waters of rare beauty called "Hilliel's Water and Hoglan's Water," easy of access, and little better than a mile from North Ness Inn. Melsetter House (the mansion of the proprietor) has one of the oldest and finest gardens in Orkney—if not the finest—and well worth a visit; from which, as from South Walls, the dreaded Pentland Firth can be seen in all its majesty and placidness, ever carrying on its bosom crafts of all sizes and of all nations. Longhope Bay is about four miles in length. Each side of its entrance is defended by a martello tower, while on the north side is a battery upon the erection of which £20,000 were spent. The Bay affords excellent harbour accommodation, and many vessels run thither for shelter. Though still the principal resort in Orkney for wind-bound vessels, its safe anchorage is not so much resorted to as formerly, owing to the vessels of the present day being better suited to remain at sea. The opening of the Caledonian Canal contributed in no small degree to decrease the craft resorting thereto. Steam communication with the mainland and the neighbouring islands would contribute in a high degree to the development of the commercial and agricultural interests of the community, as well as bringing it into closer contact with southern interests, and would afford opportunities for tourists hitherto wanting. It is contemplated that at no distant date Long-hope will have its mails conveyed by steamer, which will be a great improvement on present arrangements. Telegraphic communication has been for some time in existence, which, together with the Money Order Office and Postal Savings Bank lately established, are proving valuable and incalculable boons to the public. During the winter six months the mails leave twice a-week—viz., Tuesday and Satur-day, and during the summer six months thrice—viz., Tuesday, Thursday, and Saturday. Whilst here, the visitor may cross to

Flotta,

Which is about three miles distant from Walls. Flotta was disjoined from Walls in 1882, and is now a *quoad sacra* parish. There is only one Church on the island, which is situated at Kirkhope Bay. Near this, are the remains of the old Church in which the Presbyteries of the North of Scotland were in the habit of meeting. The Church was surrounded by three crosses, and one of these may be seen in a wall adjoining the churchyard. On the island of Flotta there are two burial mounds or *tumuli*.

We can now take boat, and go in the course of the mail steamer, (which passes Flotta every day), get picked up, and proceed to Scapa, Kirkwall, which is a short but very enjoyable sail.

APPENDICES.

APPENDIX A.

Ruined Churches in Orkney.
BY SIR H. DRYDEN, BART., HON. MEM. SOC. ANTIQ. SCOT.
(From " The Orcadian " 1867, 1868, and 1871.)

KIRKWALL, CHURCH OF ST . OLA.

This church stands in Bridge Street Lane, and is now a carpenter's shop and warehouse, the property of Mrs John Reid. It formerly was inclosed in a "close" or court, and was once converted into a " poorhouse," from which the close was called " poorhouse close." It has been so much mutilated in its several conversions that little can be stated of its original style and arrangement.

It stands about W. by S. and E. by N. It consists of one parallelogram 35 ft. by 18 ft. inside. The S. side abuts on the lane, and a house is attached to the W. end, from which house into the chapel a modern doorway has been cut.

The S. wall is 2 ft. 11 in. thick, the W. 3 ft. 6 inches.

The original entrance is on the S., 17 ft. from the exterior W. angle. It is 3 ft. 5 in. wide, with a semi-circular head and continuous mouldings, of a hollow, ornamented with four leaved flowers and a filleted roll, like many of the mouldings in the Cathedral, except as to the flowers. When the street was paved about 30 years ago the ground was raised, the jambs were covered up 9 inches, two stones were inserted just below the impost and the arch raised. What the height of the side-walls was is not now evident. They are now about 20 ft. above the original floor at the entrance. Probably the ridge was about 24 ft. high.

The E. end has no trace of an original window, but a modern one has been inserted. In the S. wall near the E. angle is a modern window, but probably in the place of an original one. The other original windows cannot be traced. Probably there was a step at 10 ft. or 11 ft from the E. end, and perhaps a screen. A few feet E. of the entrance inside was a stoup or piscina. In the N. wall near the E. angle remains an ambry 1 ft. 4¾ ins. wide, 2 ft. 1 in. high, and 1 ft. 3½ ins. recessed. The head is an ogee arch under a hood moulding, and it is flanked by buttresses with finials. The bottom of this ambry is 5 ft. 1 in. above what appears to have been the original level of the floor. The moulding of this resembles that of the entrance except in having no flowers.

In the E. wall near the S. angle is a smaller ambry, also ogee headed and less ornate, the bottom of which is 2 ft. 6 in. above the floor. The use of the ogee is very rare in Scotland. The only curves of that kind in St. Magnus are in fragments of Bishop Tulloch's tomb.

South of the chapel in what is now the lane were found in forming the lane, grave-stones and human bones. Close by the chapel was lying, in 1855, a stone, having on it sculptured in relief, apparently a shield, under a mitre, but too much defaced to be recognised, and below the shield, "Robertvs . . .," and a date or letters illegible. Bishop Robert Reid held the see from 1540 to the Reformation ; and as the mouldings (especially the four-leaved flower and the ogee arch) point to the 15th century, perhaps the chapel may be a late example of the style, and be assigned to him. His coat of arms is a stag's head cabossed.

The parish in which the town of Kirkwall is situated is that of St. Ola, and it is certain that in this part of the town was the Parish Church, dedicated to the great warrior saint of Norway—St. Ola.

The fact of burials having been made close to this building, makes it probable that this was the parish church ; not a chapel of ease or of private endowment. Of course this building was not the *first* parish church, though it may have occupied the site of the first, and probably did so.

It was probably after the constitution of Kirkwall as a royal burgh, about 1470, that the Cathedral became practically the parish church, and St. Ola became merged in Kirkwall. The name Kirkwall (Church-bay) being wholly Norse, is some evidence that the name was caused by a Norse, not a Culdee church. The situation could hardly fail to induce settlement of the Norsemen there. In the name Egilsey we have inference of a different origin as will be hereafter mentioned. But supposing that the conjecture as to the name of Kirkwall is correct, it does not prove that there was not a Culdee church there. See the first article of " Ancient Orcadia " in the *Orcadian* of May 26. 1860.

Planned 1855.

Note by Geo. Petrie, Kirkwall, Corr. Mem. Soc. Antiq. Scot.

According to Jo. Ben, whose description of Orkney is dated 1529, St. Ola's Church was reduced to ashes by the English, probably during one of their many raids on the islands about that time. One of the raids was on 13th August 1502. As apparently corroborative of Sir Henry Dryden's conjecture, that St. Ola's Church was the parish church before the Cathedral was so styled, an old charter in my possession proves that not only was the church known as St. Ola's Kirk, but it had " St. Olaf's kirkyard," " St. Olaf's burn," and " St. Olaf's brig," in its vicinity. I think the fair inference from this is, that a church built here during the early part of the Norsemen's possession of the islands was dedicated with its " kirkyard " to St. Olaf. The name soon extended to the neighbouring small stream or burn, and the " brig " by which it was crossed ; and in the course of time embraced a considerable portion of the surrounding country. It is very probable that St. Ola's Kirk occupied the same site on which stood the older building, from which the town was named by the Norsemen, Kirkevaag (Kirk-bay), which was anciently pronounced " Kirkwaw," and appears in that form in some old documents in my possession.

The fact that St. Ola's Church had been destroyed in the beginning of the 16th century, renders it almost certain that Sir Henry Dryden must be correct in attributing the erection of the church, of which there are considerable remains, to Bishop Robert Reid, as the style of architecture, as shown by Sir Henry, is in keeping with the period to which he supposes the building to belong.

The charter I have referred to, is dated at " Kirkwall in Orkney ye last of July " 1580, and granted by " John Tailyor and Henric Tailyor brether germane, and airis to our umqle fayir '(father) Andro Tailyor, to our weil-be-louit friend Magnus Paplay " of " All and Haill ane hall, ane seller, ane chalm. yr. aboue wyt. yaird and pt. nents yr. to p.tene.g quhatsomeuir lyand adjacent to Sanct Olaiffis brig, Kirk and Kirkyaird of the samy. having on the Est pt. y.roff the housses p.tenc.g to Symound Beatoun ; on the West pt. Sanct Olaiffis Kirk and yaird of the samy.; on the South pt. the housses p.tene.g to Johnne Vysshart and Sant Olaffis burne yr. betuixt and to ye North pt. Sanct Katerins quoyis.

CHURCH AT ORPHIR, ORKNEY.

This highly interesting fragment stands near the E. end of the parish church, and probably the reason why it has not obtained that notice which it deserves is that the larger and most interesting part of it was destroyed before 1758 to build or enlarge the present parish church. It consisted originally of a circular nave and apsidal chancel added to its E. part. The chancel remains, but only 9 ft. on each side of it of the circular nave. Fortunately we have a short record of its size and form in Sinclair's Stat. Ac. xix. 417, quoted in Wilson's Pre. An. 598. It is there stated, "In the churchyard are the remains of an ancient building called the Girth-House, to which great antiquity is ascribed. It is a rotundo, 18 ft. in diameter and 20 ft. high, open at top; and on the E. side is a vaulted concavity where probably the alter stood, with a slit in the wall to admit the light; two thirds of it have been taken down to repair the parish church, &c." In the translation of Torfœus by the Rev. A. Pope, is this note by the translator, (page 108), who visited Orphir in 1758. "The temple of Orphir or Gerth-House was a rotundo 22 feet in diameter, and 61 feet perpendicular wall above ground. The cupola, with the open for the light, was of an elegant cast, and the light was all from the open and lighted the house sufficiently. There was a small slit in the east side for light to the priest who stood in a niche elegantly done. The work was very firm; and though at that time there was a breach made in order to get stones to repair the parish kirk, yet the stones crumbled to pieces before they could be loosed," &c.

In the *Orcadian*, July 1861, is an account of this church by Mr G. Petrie. It is there stated that the present parish church was erected in 1829. (See also his notice of the ruins, in the Archæol. Journal 1861, No. 71, p. 226-230.)

It is evident that the E. wall of the parish church could not have co-existed with the old nave, for the new church stands on part of it.

From these several statements we must infer that part of the old church was pulled down before 1758 to build or enlarge, not to repair, the parish church, and possibly a farther portion pulled down in 1829.

We must understand the "cupola" to be a conical roof, and "the open for the light" to be a glazed lantern on it; which, however, was probably not original. "Open at top," in Sinclair, must refer to this lantern. The frame work of it must have been of wood as at Ely.

The curvature of the two parts of the nave wall still remaining gives an interior diameter of about 19 ft., thus corroborating the diameters given by Pope and Sinclair. Neither of these persons had seen the church perfect; and the differences in the measures given by them show that their informants did not speak from exact data. The "61 ft. perpendicular wall" is a gross mistake either of printer, or translator, or his informant. Even the "20 ft. high" seems over the mark, though this may be a loose approximation to the height of the side walls.

Supposing the preceding conjectures as to the shape of the roof to be correct, the top of the "fleche" surmounting the lantern would be about 40 ft. Then, supposing that Pope was told that the height was 41 ft. and the height of the side walls 20 ft. he might have added them together.

The diameter was less open to error than the height. One writer, however, might give the outer diameter and the other the inner.

It is built of yellow Orphir freestone. The nave walls are 3 feet 9 ins. thick, well built; and probably the entrance was at the W. as in the other round churches.

It is highly improbable that Pope is right in stating that "the light was all from the open"—that is, that there were no windows in the nave walls. Probably there were 4 single lights.

The chancel, which is little more than the apse, is 7 feet 2 inches wide, and 7 feet 9 inches deep or long inside, with wall 2 feet 8 inches thick. The arch into it is semi-circular, and forms part of a plain unribbed vault, as at St. Margaret's Chapel at Edinburgh. The impost of the vault arch is 6 feet 5 in. above what appears to have been the floor, and the top consequently 10 feet 6 inches high. Outside the vault was originally probably a solid stone roof, the apex of which was about 14 feet from the floor. This height (supposing also that there was a step at the chancel-arch) would oblige the walls of the nave to be about 15 feet high. The chancel has no buttresses. There is one window in the chancel, in the E. end, 2 feet 5 in. by 10¼ in., clear opening with jambs splayed inward to 1 foot 8 in. wide. The outer edges are chamfered and the head semi-circular. The impost is at the same level as of vault. It has a groove for glass.

A stone lying down appears to be part of a stoup.

The exterior width of the chancel is half the exterior width of the nave.

On the S. side of the nave is the trace of a building in the form of a parallelogram, and other indications of buildings. Pope states that before his visit in 1758, large foundations had been found in digging earth for the Bow of Orphir, near the Gerth-House.

The " 4 round churches " of Britain are, Cambridge, consecrated in 1101, Northampton, probably shortly before 1115, Maplestead, 1118, and London, 1185. (Britton Arch. Ant. Vol. 1, North Arch. Soc., Part 10, 1860. Billings Temple Church.) To these must be added the small Norman chapel in Ludlow Castle, and we may safely add as a 6th, Orphir. The church of the Holy Sepulchre at Jerusalem was the type of all, and the Crusades were the means of importing the form into Britain. In conjecturing the date of Orphir we may take into account that there was a palace of the Earl Haco (son of Paul I.), at Orphir, according to Torfœus. He went to the Holy Land and back, and died in 1103. The same writer describes the palace of Earl Paul II. at Orphir, and states that a temple stood opposite the wall of the palace. This Earl died about 1136. If this statement is to be believed, this must be the church mentioned, and hence we get 1090—1137 as the limits within which this church was built.

Earl Ronald founded the Cathedral in 1138, and soon after went to the Holy Land, accompanied, of course, by some of his high officers. He died in 1158. We may fairly conclude that this round church had some connection with one of these expeditions. As Earl Ronald needed all his money for the Cathedral, we cannot suppose that he had any hand in building Orphir, but it is not improbable that some one of his wealthier followers built it, and we may, from the dates of the other churches and these facts, fix on 1090–1160, as limits of the date of its erection.

In the Edinburgh Museum is a stone article, presented by D. Balfour, Esq., found at this church. It is circular, 4¼ in. diameter, ¾ in. thick, with a small square hole in centre. Its use is not evident.

Planned 1855.

CHAPEL ON THE BROUGH OF DEERNESS.

The brough is on the E. coast of Deerness, and measures on the top about 400 feet N. and S., by 240 feet E. and W. It is separated from the mainland on the S.W. by a narrow ravine or "geo," which is almost wet at high water.

The Brough is highest on the N., and at that part is about 90 or a hundred feet high. The coast hereabouts is steep and rocky. The use of the word *brough* for a detached rock, when *no fort* is placed on it, is not unfrequent.

The chapel is near the centre of the brough, inclosed in a yard 57 feet by 45 feet, of which only the foundation remains. The entrance into this is not evident. The chapel is a parallelogram, 24 feet 5 in. by 17 feet 4 in. outside. The W. wall 3 ft. 2 in., and the others 3 feet 11 in. thick. Only about 4 feet 6 in, and 5 feet in height remain above ground. It stands nearly true E. and W., the W. end facing a little S. of W. It is built of clay slate from 1 foot to 3 feet long, and 2 to 7 in. thick, now much covered with yellow lichen. It has only one doorway, which is in the W. end, and apparently was only 2 feet wide ; but the W. wall is irregular, and appears to have been altered and repaired. The upper part of the doorway is gone, but probably it was square headed with a stone lintel. The jambs are not splayed, and have no rebate for a door, nor is there any bar hole. See account of doorway in chapel on Brough of Birsay for notice of this point. By digging at the W. doorway it appeared probable that the floor inside was about 6 feet below top of sill of E. window, but the level is uncertain, as the interior is much covered with debris.

Apparently there was only one window, which is in the E. end. The top is gone so that it is doubtful whether it was flat or arched. One jamb is gone and the other somewhat mutilated, but 1 foot 9 in. in height of it remains. The window had a clear opening of 1 foot 3 in. with jambs splayed inside, to 3 feet 6 in. in width. It appears to have had the outer 11 in. of the jambs parallel, and to have contained glass. On a part of the E. wall is built a beacon used for the survey.

In the N. wall, near E. end, is an ambry 2 feet 4 in. wide, not less that 2 feet 4 in. high (top is gone) and 1 foot 11 in. recessed. It has no traces of having had a door. See account of the chapel on the Brough of Birsay hereafter. Supposing the floor to have been 6 feet below sill of E. window, probably the side-walls were about 8 feet high, and the points of the gables about 18 feet from floor. The roof was probably of large slabs of stone along the eaves and above them, either of smaller slabs or of " divots " fastened down with " simmons " as on houses.

The external length is equal to the diagonal of the square of the width. About 35 yards S. of the chapel is a tank or well.

On the S. edge of the brough are stones which appear to have once formed a wall, and at this point is the entrance from the " geo."

Spread over the top of the brough are foundations of at least 18 huts. They are mostly parallelograms, of about 24 feet by 12 feet outside, and the walls 2 feet 6 in. and 3 feet thick. These were for the use of devotees who used this as a place of pilgrimage.

A survey of our coasts and lakes will show how strong a partiality existed in early times for selecting as sites for churches and monastic establishments small islands, isolated rocks, or promontories difficult of access—for instance, the two St. Michaels mounts, Lindisfarn, Iona, Irelands eye, Inisfallen, &c. Nor was this taste for isolation peculiar to the coasts. We find throughout Europe, and indeed in the East also, numbers of peaks difficult of access, bearing such buildings. The Brough of Deerness and the Brough of Birsay are good examples.

Planned 1866.

CHURCH ON THE BROUGH OF BIRSAY.

The brough contains about 40 acres, and is separated on the E. from the mainland by a rocky channel, which is about 150 yards wide and dry at low water. The surface of the brough slopes down from a high cliff on the W., to a cliff of about 20 ft. high on the E. The chapel is about 50 yards from the shore at the point nearest to the mainland. It is enclosed in a yard about 33 yards E. and W., by 27 yards N. and S., of which the wall is destroyed. At the edge of the cliff are traces of a wall. The chapel consists of nave, chancel, and apse—all well defined and all apparently built at the same time. The material is grey whinstone, and no traces of freestone dressings appear. It stands nearly E. and W., but the W. end facing a little to the N. of W.

The extreme exterior length is 57 ft., and extreme width 21 ft. 3 in.

The W. wall is 3 ft. 8 in. thick ; the N. and S. walls of nave and aisles 2 ft. 9 ins., the wall of apse 2 ft. 4 ins. There were no buttresses.

The interior is filled with debris to the depth of about 6 ft. 2 ins. above the floor, and the exterior to about the same depth. Partial excavations were made for this plan. Of the W. end only 3 feet in height of wall remains ; of the N. wall a little more, and of S. wall a little less ; of the N. wall of chancel 8 ft. 6 in. ; of S. wall of chancel about 2 ft. ; of the apse about 2 ft. 4 ins. The nave is 28 ft. 3 ins. by 15 ft. 6 ins. inside. The only entrance to the church is in the W. end, 3 ft. 8 ins. wide. The jambs are parallel without any chamfer, and there is no rebate for a door nor appearance of hinges ; and original plaster remains on the jamb down to the sill and all across it. There is no appearance of the insertion of a wooden frame. This mode of making jambs of doorways is to be seen at Lybster in Caithness, Wyre, Linton in Shapinsay, Uya in Shetland, and in some of the oratories in Ireland, &c. (See Petric's Round Towers and Wilson's Prehis. Annals.) Were there doors in these doorways, and, if so, where placed and how hung ? It is known that in many cottages in old times the door was an animal's hide hung across the opening, and probably this may have been the case in these unrebated church entrances.

Possibly this plain jamb may be an evidence of antiquity ; though Egilsey and Kirk of the Ness in Yell have the usual form of jamb. Probably this doorway was surmounted by a semi-circular arch, though many of the ruder chapels had square-headed doorways with a large stone lintel as at Lybster, in Reay parish, in Caithness. There are very few instances of the passage between a nave and chancel being square-headed. Where there is a semi-circular arch on plain jambs, as in the doorways before mentioned, and in some chancel arches, as at Linton, Shapinsay ; Kirk of the Ness, Yell ; Wyre, &c. ; there is generally a peculiarity which may be mentioned here— the feet of the arch are set back on the jambs at the imposts 2 or 3 inches on each side. This was probably to support the centre on which the arch was built, instead of supporting it by props from the floor.

In the N.E. and S.E. corners are two circular spaces 5 ft. 6 ins. in diameter, the S. one of which contains a freestone stair step, and the N. one some broken stone. Probably both were stair cases ; but how high they reached, to what they led, and what was the superstructure we can only conjecture. One or both may have led to turrets or to priests' rooms over the chancel arch, or chancel or nave. We cannot suppose a rood-loft to have existed here. The support of the W. side of the stairs is now gone, but we must suppose that a block of masonry existed which included the circle of the staircase. Against this, the *seat* on the S. apparently runs past the spot at which it should have stood, and there are no decisive traces of a junction in the N. and S. walls. There is no other solution of the difficulty. This very massive separation between nave and chancel is probably unique. M'Cormac's chapel at Cashel has a turret and a chamber in nearly the same positions as these staircases ; but the construction in that case is clear. (See Petrie's "Round Towers.")

A stone seat, 1 ft. 2 ins. high, and 1 ft. 2 ins. wide ran all round the nave—at least it was traced at W. doorway and at the E. end of the S. wall of the nave. The roof was probably of tie beam construction, and covered with stone slabs.

The entrance to the chancel is 4 ft. 3 ins. wide, of which 4 ft. in height of the jambs remain. These are 3 ft. 7 ins. thick from W. to E., but, if the construction was that suggested above, the jambs were 7 ft. from W. to E., including an entrance into each turret 2 ft. wide. The entrance to the chancel was probably surmounted by a semi-circular arch of whinstone, plastered, about 8 ft. or 9 ft. high to the apex, with string-course caps 4 or 5 inches deep. The angles were not chamfered.

There is a step in this entrance of only 2 ins., and from that to the E. end of the apse was flush originally. The pavement is of flag stones. This low position of the original altar is peculiar.

The chancel is 10 ft. 9 ins. E. and W., and 10 ft. 3 ins. inside. Only one window remains, which is in the N. wall of chancel, and this has lost its lintel. The clear opening was 3 ft. by 10½ ins., with, as stated, a square head. The window has an internal and external splay, each widening to 1 ft. 10½ ins. This form is peculiar. There was probably a frame, fixed in the narrow part of the opening, containing glass. In this wall, just E. of the window, and lower, is a square ambry 3 ft. high by 2 ft. 8 ins. wide, and 1 ft. 11 ins. recess. The use of so large an ambry is not evident. The bottom of it is only 2 ft. above floor. There is no appearance of its having had doors. In the N.E. part of the nave of Enhallow chapel is a similar recess, and one in the same position as this in the chapel on the Brough of Deerness. It is possible, but not probable, that these were Easter sepulchres. In the Kirk of the Ness, N. Yell, is a larger one. Of the S. wall of the chancel so little remains that nothing can be stated as to window, piscina, or sedile.

It is remarkable that the floor was originally level to the end of the apse, and no elevation given to the altar, which was probably at the chord of the apse ; but in later times they built a reredos which *blocked off* the apse, and then they appear to have made steps to the altar. Some parts of the altar remains. It appears to have been 4 ft. 1 in. by 2 ft 7 ins. Possibly the reredos did not reach many feet high, so that the upper part of the apse appeared over it.

As there were no buttresses it is not likely that the chancel was vaulted. The roof was probably of tie-beam construction or of rafters coupled half way up, as in cottages; and covered as the nave roof. It is probable that the apse was vaulted and the arch into it may be conjectured to have been 10 ft. high, and semi-circular, and to have formed part of a plain vault, as at Orphir and St. Margaret's Chapel at Edinburgh. The ground plan is somewhat in the form of a horse-shoe internally. Probably there was a small window in E. end, and this must have been at a lower level than the one on the N.

The interior of the nave is of the proportion of the vesica piscis. The width of the chancel is less than of the nave by the thickness of the side walls. The interior of the chancel is square. It is stated in Barry (Hist. Ork., p. 34) to have been dedicated to St. Peter, and to have been a place of pilgrimage. The writer was informed that many years ago a skewer was found with a skull outside the chapel. This was probably the pin of a winding sheet.

There can be little hesitation in assigning this church to about 1100. It is recorded that Earl Thorfinn built Christ's Church in Birsay, and that the body of St. Magnus was buried there. It appears probable that if St. Peter's had been built as long after his death as his canonization it would have been dedicated to him. Even, if it had been built in memory of St. Magnus before his canonization, and dedicated to some other saint, probably the dedication would have been changed after his canonization. As it is recorded that Thorfinn built Christ's Church, it is probable that if he had built St. Peter's, it would have been recorded also. It is more probable that it was built by his second son, Erlend, the father of St. Magnus.

This church bears considerable resemblance to Old Bewick, Northumberland, figured in Muir's Sketch; to Moccas and Kilpeck in Herefordshire, and to St. Margaret's Chapel, Edinburgh.

Mr Leask of Boardhouse, has recently made an excavation in the church, to determine if possible whether foundations exist of the walls supposed to have inclosed the W. sides of the circular recesses. He found none, and found plaster on the N. wall of the nave, where the supposed wall should have joined. Possibly the supposed wall was taken down during the time the chapel was used. He found in the N. wall of the nave, at 5 feet W. of the angle of the recess, an entrance 2 feet 4 in. wide. The position is very unusual.

Planned 1866.

CHURCH ON WYRE.

This stands on a flat piece of ground about the middle of the island, in a walled burial ground, still used. The chapel has no roof, and is much filled up with rubbish. Large parts of the S. wall have tumbled, as well as smaller portions of other walls.

It is built of grey whinstone, without any freestone dressings. The stones average about 1 foot 6 in. long by about 5 inches thick. It consists of chancel and nave, with a door at W. end—all built at the same time. The extreme exterior length is 35 feet 10 inches, and width 18 feet 4 inches. It stands W. by S. and E. by N. The nave is 19 feet 2 inches by 12 feet 10 inches inside.

The W. entrance is 2 feet 6 inches wide at bottom, with semi-circular head, the feet of which are set back at the impost 2½ inches on each side. This mode of putting the arch on was probably done to give a support to the centre on which the arch was built. The jambs are parallel, 3 feet 2 inches thick, and have no rebate for a door, nor any traces of there having been one. (See account of Chapel on the Brough of Birsay.) There is no cap. The impost is 4 feet 11 inches above original stone sill. The whole interior is from 1 foot 6 inches to 2 feet deep in rubbish.

The W. wall is 3 feet 2 in. thick, the N. and S. about 3 feet.

There are no windows on the N. or W. of the nave. There are 2 on the S. side, but only one of these appears original. This has a clear opening of 1 foot 10 in. by 8 inches, with a flat head. The jambs splay inward to 2 feet 3 in. in width. The outer edges are broken, so that it is uncertain whether it had an external chamfer.

The upper part of the side walls is in many places destroyed, but as far as can be now ascertained, the top of the nave walls was 11 feet 5 inches above the sill of W. door. The chancel walls were only 4 or 5 inches lower.

The upper part of all the gables is gone.

The chancel arch is exactly like the W. entrance in every way. The jambs are 3 feet thick. A springer of the gable coping remains at the N.E. angle, 1 foot wide, 7 or 8 inches thick, and of a foot projection. In 1852 the springer at the S.W. angle was existing. The chancel is 7 feet 10 inches by 7 feet 2 inches inside.

There is one window on the S. which appears to have been round headed, and 2 feet 7 inches by 11 inches. The jambs splay inward to 2 feet 11 in. width. The outer edges are broken, but there seems to have been an external splay. There is no ambry and no trace of altar or altar place.

The springers of the gable-coping remain at the S.E. and N.E. angles. These are 1 foot wide and about 8 inches thick, and project 1 foot.

The roofs of nave and chancel were either of tie-beam construction or of rafters coupled half-way up, and covered with stone slates.

My conjectural restoration makes the ridge of the nave roof 19 feet above the sill of the W. entrance. This chapel closely resembles in size and form the chapel at Lybster in Caithness, described by Muir in " Eccl. Sketch of Caithness and Orkney," 1861, but in that chapel the W. entrance is square headed. The entrance from the nave to the chancel is also square headed. Muir makes Lybster chancel stand to the N. of the nave, but it is in the usual position. Probably Wyre Chapel is of the 12th or 13th century, but the characteristics are not decisive enough to approximate more closely to its date. It is called " Cubberow " chapel from its vicinity to Cubberow Castle.

The exterior length of the nave is equal to the diagonal of the square of its exterior width. The chancel is nearly square.

Planned 1866.

CHURCH ON ENHALLOW.

This church, till lately, was unknown for many years, having been converted long ago into a cottage. On the small island Enhallow (the holy island) on the S.W. slope of it, and about 200 yards from the shore, is a cluster of 4 cottages, in which four families lived. In 18— fever broke out among them, and the owner, Mr Balfour, took the whole off the island, and pulled the roofs off the cottages. In this clearance the church was discovered. Having been altered and added to in its church time, and having since been altered and added to in its domestic time, its history is very puzzling.

It is of grey whinstones, mostly from 1 foot to 2 feet long (average 1 foot 6 inches), and 6 to 2 inches thick. The exterior length is 52 feet 8 inches, and the extreme width 23 feet 4 inches. It stands nearly exactly E. and W. The nave is 20 feet 7 in. by 12 feet inside. On the W. of this and entered through a round-headed arch, 4 feet 3 in. wide, with parallel jambs 2 feet 8 inches thick, is a building 7 feet 9 inches and 7 feet 5 inches inside, with walls 2 feet 7 inches thick, without any doorway to the outside, and with only one small square window to the S., perhaps not original. It is in the position of a tower, but it is not likely that a tower of that size would have been added to so small a church, and the walls are too thin. The size and character of the arch into it are against the notion that it was a priest's room, supposing the room to be co-temporary with the arch. So little remains of the side walls that with regard to the windows and roof and height, we are left to conjecture. There is no appearance of its having been higher than the nave. It most resembles a chancel on the W., and there is in Uyea, Shetland, a chapel with a building apparently original, in that position. If we may suppose that the W. arch was the *original* entrance to the church, and that the S. doorway was of later date, then this building may have been a sacristy, co-temporary with the S. doorway. The floor of the late cottage was about 1 foot 3 inches above what appears to have been the floor of the W. arch, which is 5 feet 5 in. below the top of cap. The N. wall is 2 feet 10 in. thick, and the S. wall 2 feet 6 in. They are about 10 feet 6 inches or 11 feet above the supposed sill of the W. arch.

The S. doorway is of ecclesiastical date, even if the jambs are not original. The N. doorway is perhaps domestic, though resembling that on S. They have the usual rebate and wooden frames fixed in them, and have lately been the doors of the cottage.

The heads are square. Probably at the beginning of the domestic period the S. one was altered in some degree, and the N. one made or altered. If the building at the W. end was the original chancel, these entrances are not co-temporary with *that*, being in wrong position for that arrangement.

It is not certain whether the present chancel on the E. is co-temporary with the nave, or whether there was an earlier one or none ; but the present chancel arch is clearly an addition of a much later date than the nave. It is 4 feet 1 in. wide, pointed, has red freestone caps chamfered ; and the mark of insertion is clear on the N. side of it. It will be seen that the nave is 11 feet 3 in. wide at W. end, and 12 feet at E., and in the S.E. corner there is a slight projection and roughness. This may be the junction of a former S. wall of the nave which got out of repair, or it may be the junction of the jamb of the chancel arch. When the chapel came to be used for a cottage it was divided into 2 stories.

On the N. is one window, square-headed, 2 feet by 1 foot 2 in. clear, with splayed jambs, but without freestone dressings or external chamfer, and in N.E. corner is an ambry 3 feet 9 in. by 3 feet 9 in., and 1 foot 6 in. recess. The bottom 3 feet 6 in. above the original floor. The position is peculiar.

On the S. is a window like that on the N., and 3 small ambries, perhaps one or all domestic.

The windows and doors on the N. side of the nave and chancel are higher than on S. side, owing to the slope of the ground.

The chancel is 12 feet 8 in. by 8 feet 9 in. inside, set out symmetrically with the nave. When it was made domestic a door-way was cut in the N. wall. For some reason the upper part of the S. wall was pulled down, and a casing put *outside* the lower part. A fire-place and chimney were made in the E. wall, and a new face put outside the whole E. end, including the added piece on the S.; for no break or junction is visible outside the E. end. On the N. is one window 2 feet by 1 foot clear, with splayed jambs, but no freestone dressings, and no external chamfer. (See account of windows in Egilsey.) To the E. of it is a small ambry. The window and the ambry on the N. are on a higher level than on the S.

When the casing was added on the S., the window was shifted out or a lintel put in the added piece. Red freestone quoins and 2 sills (or possibly one, a square head) are lying near, and the jambs of the S. window are much broken. Probably this sill, jamb stones, and head formed the S. window, and are co-temporary with the chancel arch, having, perhaps, supplanted a window like that on the N .

Outside the S. door of nave is a square addition, measuring 8 feet 1 in. by 7 feet 7 in. inside, now only 6 feet high, containing a radiating stair of 5 freestone steps. The W. wall of it is 3 feet, and the S. and E. 2 feet 3 in. There is no evidence of what this was, or led to, but the building certainly is ecclesiastical by the character of the work. The entrance to it from outside is on the E. Perhaps the stair led to a priest's room or parvise over the porch, which, however, must have been very small ; or it led to a bell turret. There are several jamb stones of red freestone, belonging to a doorway lying about, and one (apparently in its proper position), is in the jamb of the outer entrance of this porch. This makes it probable that this building is co-temporary with chancel arch. The red freestone window jambs, above mentioned, may have come out of this porch. Whatever the upper part of this porch was, the roof must have been higher than the eaves of the nave.

Plaster, apparently ancient, remains on the S. wall of chancel lower part—on jambs of N. window of chancel, on E. side of the chancel arch, in the ambry on N. side of the nave.

The roof was either of tie-beam arrangement, or of rafters, coupled half-way up, and covered with stone slates or " divots." The ridge of the nave roof was about 18 feet above sill of W. arch.

The general history may be thus conjectured. In the 11th or 12th century a chapel was built of nave and chancel at the E. end of the nave, and an entrance in the W.

end of the nave. In the 14th century a new chancel arch was inserted, N. and S. doorways made, sacristy built at the W. end, and a porch and parvise made outside the S. doorway. After it became domestic, the changes before described were made in the chancel. At a later date other additions were made.

If we suppose that the W. building is the original *chancel*, the original *entrance* was in the place now occupied by the chancel arch.

The proportion of the inside of the nave is that of the "vesica piscis"—the width to the length as the base of an equilateral triangle to the length of 2 such triangles on opposite sides of that base, and the internal length of the chancel is equal to the diagonal of the square of the internal width.

Barry mentions a tradition that neither rats, mice, nor cats will live on the island, which tradition agrees with the name of the island.

Planned 1866.

CHAPEL AT LINTON IN SHAPINSAY.

The chapel is near the shore at the S.E. part of the island. It consists of nave and chancel, and stands nearly exactly E. and W. The extreme length is 35 feet 9 inches, and the width 19 feet 5 inches. About 7 feet in height of the E. end of the nave, including the arch into the chancel, remains, but of the rest only about 2 feet and 3 feet remains. It is built of whin stone without any freestone dressings.

The nave is 18 feet by 13 feet 7 in. inside. The walls are 3 feet thick.

The entrance is in the S. wall near the W. angle, differing in this point from most of the early chapels, and is 2 feet 8 inches wide with parallel unrebated jambs. (See observations on these entrances in notes on the Brough of Birsay.) The upper part of the entrance is gone, but probably it was a semi-circular arch. Nothing can be stated of the windows. The chancel arch is semi-circular, of rough stone, 3 feet wide, with plain parallel jambs, and the arch is set back on the jambs at the impost, which is about 5 feet 6 in. high from the supposed floor of the nave. The inside is much filled with rubbish. It is uncertain whether there was a step at the chancel arch. The chancel is 7 feet 6 in. by 7 feet inside, narrower than the nave by the thickness of the walls. The N. and S. walls are 2 feet 10 in. thick, and the E. wall 3 feet 4 in. Only about 2 feet in height of the E. wall remains; though within the memory of man the E. gable was standing and a cross on it.

Nothing can be stated of the windows. The exterior length of the nave, and the interior width are in the proportion of the vesica piscis. The chancel is nearly square.

This chapel bears close resemblance in form and size to Wyre chapel; and is probably about the same date. It is supposed by the owner that Linton farm formed part of St. Catherine's lands, and that this chapel was dedicated to that Saint.

Planned 1846 and 1851.

CHURCH ON EGILSEY.

The island on which this church stands is about 3 miles N. and S. and 1 mile E. and W. The church is on the W. side, near the Howa Sound which separates Egilsey from Rousay, and is a conspicuous object from all sides, as the island has no prominent points, and the church is on the highest ground.

The flood tide runs from N.W. to S.E. There is a landing-place at the S. point and on W. side, but not at N. point. The name Egilsey or Egilshay is derived from an ancient form of the Gaelic word *eaglais* a church (derived from ecclesia), with the Norse addition of *ey* an island.

Professor Munch infers that the Norsemen found a church here and called the island after it; and if this is the case the date of the erection of the church is put very far back, unless we suppose this to be a *second* church. It was dedicated to St. Magnus; but this might be a second dedication and probably was so. At the end of this article are further remarks on this point. The church is complete except the roofs and the upper part of the tower, and was used up to about 18— as the place of worship. It consists of a chancel, nave, and tower, at the W. end of the nave, and stands nearly exactly E. and W.

The only alterations which appear to have been made in the building are 2 or 3 windows. The ground plan shows a proportion which, if not intententional, is singular. If 4 circles of the exterior diameter of the tower are laid down in a line, and the first occupied by the tower, the second and third fill the inside of the nave, and the fourth takes in the chancel, including the side walls, but excluding the E. wall. The whole is of grey whinstone without any freestone dressings, and has become very picturesque in colour from the rich gray lichen on some parts and bright yellow lichen on others.

The masonry is chiefly in courses, but the size of the stones very irregular, some being as large as 4 feet long and 1 foot 6 in. deep. The interstices are filled with very small stones. Here and there irregular blocks are inserted The whole is built with mortar.

The extreme length is 62 feet 9 inches, and the extreme width is 24 feet 7 inches.

The nave is 29 feet 9 in. by 15 feet 6 inches inside. The N. and S. walls are 3 feet thick. On the N. and S., opposite each other, are 2 doorways 2 feet 6 in. wide. These have round arched heads and rebated jambs without chamfers. On the N. side of the nave is a window 3 feet 3 in. high and 8¼ inches wide at the outside of the wall with semi-circular head. The jambs are splayed inwards to 2 feet 9 in. wide. On the S. is a similar window. It is to be observed that these windows have no external chamfer—that is, the outer edges of the jambs are acute angles. This peculiarity is found in early Irish churches. (See Petrie's Early Round Towers, p. 162, 181-5.) They were not originally glazed, but probably had a frame fitted into them, when required, covered with parchment. On this S. side are two windows, not original—one close to the E. wall and low down, the other high up over the S. doorway. The side walls are about 15 feet 4 in. high from the floor, equal to the internal width of the nave.

On the W. of the nave is the tower, which is circular, 14 feet 10½ in. diameter externally, and 7 feet 8 in. diameter internally. An arch 2 feet 5 in. wide leads from the nave into it. The jambs are 3 feet 7 in. thick, and the head is semi-circular. The tower appears to have been built with the nave, although the stones in the tower are on the average smaller than those in the nave; which difference may be accounted for by the unfitness of large stones, when not freestone, for circular work.

The tower seems to have contained 4 chambers, including the one on the ground.

Above the tower arch, at 16 feet 3 in. from the floor of the nave, but under the nave roof, is an arched opening in the tower 5 feet 4 in. high and 2 feet 3 in. wide. A similar opening is found in many early churches in England; the use of which is not ascertained. Arches in the same position are in St. Magnus.

The nave roof appears to have been of a "square pitch"—that is, the angle at the apex is about a right angle. Of the construction of the roof we know nothing, except that it was not vaulted.

Probably all the rafters were framed in couples and the covering formed of coarse slates.

Each end of the roof is terminated by a wall 1 foot 2 in. wide, formed of corby-steps, standing up above the roof as usual. The ridge of the roof was about 25 feet above the floor. Above the roof of the nave, in the E. side of the tower, is an arched opening 4 feet 1 in. high and 1 foot 9 in. wide, and about 7 feet above this is a smaller opening, also on the E. side of the tower. The top of the tower is now about 11 feet wide and about 48 feet from the floor of the nave. It is stated that about 15 feet was taken off the top. Probably it was surmounted by a conical roof.

On the S. side and near the ground is a window, but this is a modern work. There is a small window in the second storey looking N., and a similar one in the fourth storey also looking N.

The chancel is 14 feet 11 in. by 9 feet 5½ in. inside, the side walls 2 feet 9 in. thick, and the E. wall about the same. It is roofed with a plain barrel vault, of which the semi-circular chancel arch forms part. The impost of this arch is 5 feet from the floor of the nave. Probably there was a step here or a little further E.

The pressure of the vault has forced out the jambs of the arch (that is, the side walls) and given the arch a horse-shoe form. Dr Wilson lays some stress on this peculiarity of form, taking it to be intentional, but it is purely the result of lateral pressure.

The E. end has no window. On the N. is a window 1 foot 7½ in. high and 11 in. wide at the outside, with a semi-circular head, below the impost of the vault. The jambs are splayed inward to 2 feet 1 in. in width, without an external chamfer. On the S. is a similar window. Probably, like the nave windows, they were not originally glazed.

Over the vault of the chancel is a chamber, entered from the nave by a semi-circular arch 6 feet 4 in. high, and 2 feet 2 in. wide, over the chancel arch.

It is lit by a flat-headed window in the E. end 1 foot 6 in. high. This probably served as a depository for books, muniments, &c.

It is called by the country people " grief house," and is supposed to have been a prison, &c.

The side walls of this chamber are 2 feet 4½ in. thick, and the E. wall 2 feet 7½ in.

The ridge of the chancel roof was 20 feet 9 in. above the floor of the nave.

It remains to approximate to the date of this church.

There was a church in Egilsey when St. Magnus was murdered in 1110. The attaching so large a tower to the church tends to show that it was a church of a superior order when it was built.

The style of architecture (discarding certain indications of an earlier date) prevents our assigning it to a later date than the beginning of the 12th century. When we contrast it with the Kirkwall Cathedral, begun in 1137, we are forced to give an earlier date than that to Egilsey. This opinion is corroborated by the churches at Orphir and the Brough of Birsay. The islands were conquered by the Norsemen in 876, and reconverted to Christianity in 998. The church, therefore, was probably not built between these dates. There were Christians in these islands before the arrival of the Norsemen. The name of the island, as before mentioned, is evidence that there was a church of distinction in Egilsey when they arrived.

Neale (Ecc. Notes on the Orkneys, &c.) supposes that the church to which St. Magnus fled was on the E. side of the island ; supposing Haco to have come from Birsay by the N. of Rousay to the E. of Egilsey. Haco's starting point is not certain ; but if it was Birsay he would naturally have come by the S. of Rousay to the W. of Egilsey.

There is some confusion about the Episcopal Church and residence. Barry, p. 162, quotes Torfœus as stating that Bishop William lived in Egilsey. Neale (following Barry) has made the same statement.

Torfœus twice states that the Bishop resided at Birsay.

The Saga is still more to the point, and states that at the time of St. Magnus' death William the Old was Bishop and the see was then at Birsay. But Torfœus in three or more other passages states that Bishop William *was in* Egilsey—not necessarily *residing* there.

We must understand (if Torfœus is right) that he generally *lived* in Birsay, but often officiated at Egilsey. We may thence infer that Egilsey was an important church in Bishop William's time, and that it was fixed on as the place of meeting of Haco and Magnus from being frequently the Bishop's abode. We do not, however, find the Bishop mentioned in the account of the murder of St. Magnus as adviser or mediator. (See account of the early Bishops of Orkney by Professor Munch, in Bannatyne Miscellany, vol. III., 1855.)

Wilson, in his Prehistoric Annals, p. 587, has a notice of this church, to which the reader is referred. He supposes it to be the work of Irish Christians before the expedition of Harold in 876, and to be the church which caused the Norsemen to give its present appellation to the island.

There is at all events nothing to disprove this, but if we put the tower for the moment out of the question, there is little to induce the assignment of so early a date. The absence of freestone, the round arches, the chancel vault, the small number and size of the windows, do not necessitate a date earlier than the 12th century!

The tower, then, is the feature which specially points to an earlier period. Dr Wilson apparently inclines to class this tower with the later round towers of Scotland and Ireland.

When, however, we compare it, there appears little or no resemblance except its circularity.

The round towers, with one or two exceptions, are detached buildings, though situated within a few feet of churches, have their entrances at several feet from the ground, and have jambs inclined towards each other upwards. They have other differences of construction, which, however, may be in part accounted for by the difference of the available materials.

The Irish tower, which most resembles Egilsey, is the smaller one of the two at Clonmacnoise. This is an integral part of the church, and joined to the S. E. angle of the nave. The entrance to it is on the ground, from the chancel. To this church Dr Petrie assigns the date of some years before 1000, (p. 271) In many particulars the tower at Egilsey approximates more closely to the round towers of Norfolk, which are of the 12th and 13th centuries. There is no evidence of another church in another place having existed in the island ; nor account of the *building* of any church in the island.

These, however, are very slight evidences of the antiquity of the present church.

There does not appear to be positive evidence that the Christian priests were exterminated by the Norse conquest ; though it is probable that they would fly westward. If, however, we give up the idea of its Norse origin we ought to find resemblances between it and the ancient Irish churches of the 8th, 9th, and 10th centuries. These we do find. 1st. The size of Egilsey is close on the authoritative size of the more important of the ancient churches, presuming the present foot to be about equal to the ancient Irish foot. The authorized Irish size is 60 ft. by 27 ft. ; Egilsey is 62 ft. 9 ins. and 21 ft. 7 ins. The lowness of the chancel, the chamfer or "croft" over it, the 2d chamfer in the tower, with an arch from it into the nave over the tower arch, the number and size of the windows, the peculiarity of their splays, having no exterior chamfer, the character of the masonry, all resemble the early Irish churches. On the other hand, three great criteria of an early Irish church are not found in Egilsey—the approximation of the jambs of doors and windows towards their imposts, the horizontal heads to the doorways, and the E. window. It seems, however, probable that the difference of the materials induced one of these differences. It was difficult to get in Orkney lintels strong and long enough for heads of doorways, though we find them in the broughs. The rebates in the doorways are against a very early date.

It seems on the whole fair to suppose Egilsey to have been built after the traditional Irish form, but with modifications ; and soon after the re-conversion of the islands to Christianity in 998. If built before that time we must refer it to the beginning or middle of the 9th century.

Unfortunately, Neale, when in Orkney, was unable to see this church, and has given a cut, professing to be an approximate likeness of the tower, which is very erroneous in several particulars. The etching in Muir's "Sketch" is also wrong in proportion.

In the *Oreadian* of Jan., 1855, is an account by Mr Petrie, of the finding the remains of Bishop William "the old," in the Cathedral in 1848. His bones and the chest containing them were removed when the Cathedral was re-seated in 1855. The leaden plate bearing the inscription, and a bone article (doubtless the cross handle of his walking stick) found in the chest, are now in the Edinburgh Museum.

Planned 1846.

CHURCH AT SWENDRO, ROUSAY.

This is in a grave-yard, close to the W. shore of Rousay, about a mile N. of Westness. It consists of a long parallelogram, and, but for a stoup near the door and apparently an ambry near the E. end, might be taken for a post-reformation building. It has been used till within memory. It stands about E. and W. It is 52ft. 11in. E. and W., × 14ft. 5in. N. and S. inside, and the walls are 2ft. 6in. on N. and S., 2ft. 11in. on

E., and 3ft. 8in. on the W. It is now roofless and in some parts broken. From the floor to the top of side walls is 9ft. 10in.

There is one doorway near the W. end of the S. wall. This is flat-headed and rebated, measuring 3ft. 4in. clear width.

To the W. of this doorway and low down is a window, 2ft. 11in. × 1ft. 4in., clear, flat-headed and splayed inwards and outwards. Between the window and the doorway (inside) is a recess, probably for holy water.

To the E. of the doorway is a window 3ft. 3½in. × 1ft. 4in., flat-headed and splayed as before. The head is nearly as high as the eaves.

Farther E. is another similar window.

About midway along the N. wall is a window 2ft. 1½in. × 1ft., clear opening, flat-headed, and splayed as before. The head is nearly as high as the eaves.

In the E. end is a window of which the sill is nearly as high as the eaves, 4ft. × 1ft. 2in., clear opening with flat head and splays in and out. Under this window, and across the end inside is a sort of shelf at the height of the top of the altar.

In the W. end is a window above the level of the eaves, 3ft. 5in. × 1ft. 4in.

There is a seat inside, along the W. end and part of the N. side.

The E. and W. gables are in steps, which remain tolerably entire.

The floor of the church is gone.

In the yard are numerous rough tombstones, and a few more modern.

Outside the N.W. corner of the yard is the foundation of a small strong rectangular building, which has more the appearance of a fort than a church, but close to it, as is stated, were found some carved stones of the red sandstone now at Westness, one of which appears to be the cap of an elaborate church doorway, with three shafts on each side.

Planned 1870.

CHAPEL IN WESTRAY.

This is in the "West Grave-yard," which is still used, though the chapel has been for many years a ruin. It consists of nave and chancel, and is built of the schist of the locality. According to Peterkin, it was dedicated to St. Cross.

It stands E. and W., within 2°.

The nave originally measured 19ft. E. and W., by 13ft. 4in. N. and S. inside, but was elongated long subsequently to its erection, so that latterly it was 46ft. 7in. by 13ft. 4in. inside. The original length is shown by a break in the S. wall at 24ft. 7in. from the S.E. angle of the nave, and by the position of the original doorway which, at the elongation, was stopped up. There is also a tradition that the church was enlarged, and when certain people within memory were pulling it down, an old inhabitant begged them not to "pull down the Danes' work," alluding to the chancel and eastern part of the nave. Of the elongation, little more than the foundations remain; but it is evident that there was not a door in the W. end or N. side, so that it must have been somewhere in the S. wall, between the old blocked doorway and the S.W. angle. The side walls are 3ft. thick. Of the old part of the S. wall, fortunately we have considerable part. The old doorway is nearly complete. It had plain parallel jambs without rebate 2ft. 4in. apart, a plain projecting abacus, and a semi-circular head set back at the impost. To the E. of that is a window entire. It has a semi-circular head, and measures 2ft. 7in. high, by 11½in. clear opening, with jambs splayed to the width of 1ft. 7½in.

The chancel arch remains entire. It has plain angular jambs 4ft. apart, a plain abacus of schist and a semi-circular head. The impost is 5ft. 7in. above what appears to be the old floor. The wall is 2ft. 9in. thick. The chancel is 9ft. 1in. E. and W. by 6ft. 8in. N. and S. inside. It had a cylindrical vault of which part remains. It springs from the level of the impost of the chancel arch, and is slightly set back at the impost as many of the old arches were, to give support to the centreing.

It had one window, which was in the E. end, which is now gone; but within a few years the E. gable was existing. According to an old inhabitant, the E. window was like the S. one in the nave. The vault is 1ft. 3in. thick.

In the graveyard is lying what appears to be the saddle-stone of one of the gables, of the red sandstone of Eday.

This chapel probably is of the 12th century, but possibly of the 13th.

Planned 1870.

ST. TREDWALL'S CHAPEL, PAPA WESTRAY.

This chapel is situated on a little holm, in a fresh water loch on the E. side of Papa Westray. It appears probable that a Pict's-house was constructed on this holm, and that the chapel was built on its ruins. This St. Tredwall is the same as St. Triduana, whose day in the Roman Calendar is Oct. 8. She is not mentioned by Alban Butler. The chapel was much frequented in its day, and many benefits were said to be obtained from the saint by her devotees. It is a plain parallelogram, 20ft. 3in. E. and W. by 13ft. 10in. N. and S. inside, and stands W. by S. and E. by N. There is a narrow doorway near the W. end of the S. side. Only the lower portion of the walls remains, except at N.W. angle, which measures 8 ft. high, but here we have as usual the unfortunate information that within memory the E. gable and S. wall were standing. The thickness of wall is on the N. 3ft. 11in., E. 4ft. 2in., S. 4ft. 3in., and W. 4ft. 9in.

It is stated that there was a window in the E. end, and that the doorway was flat-headed. No trace of a window remains, and only about 3ft. 6in. of the door jambs remain. These have a rebate into which a door fitted, but whether in a wooden frame or not cannot be ascertained.

The original floor appears to have been 10ft. above water level.

There is no means of assigning a date to this building ; but the difference in the thickness of the walls makes it possible that it has been altered since its first erection.

Planned 1870.

HALCRO CHAPEL, SOUTH RONALDSHAY.

This is now wholly destroyed, and even the foundations taken out, but the measures were obtained by Mr G. Petrie, so soon after the removal of the latter that the size of thickness of walls could be accurately determined.

It was a parallelogram 21ft. × 14ft. inside. The walls were 2ft. 6in. thick. The place of the doorway was not ascertained.

Planned 1870.

CHAPEL ON THE N. SHORE OF HEAD OF HOLLAND.

This is situated within a few yards of the shore, and not many feet above water level. It is only a heap of ruins, but the measures are just ascertainable. It is a parallelogram, measuring 37ft. E. and W., by 15ft. 4in. N. and S. inside. The N. and S. walls are 2ft. 6in. thick, and E. and W. ends 3ft. 3in., and are of the red sandstone of the locality. There was a door in the S. wall.

Planned 1870.

CHARACTERISTICS.

The following remarks were preceded by an account of the Ruined Churches of Shetland, and apply to the remains of both groups of islands :—

There is no cross church in Orkney, and only one in Shetland.

In Ireland there is no circular octagon or cross church, except, of course, the cathedrals and some monastic churches. There is no aisle in Orkney or Shetland.

There are no plinths or basements to any of these churches.

The doors are chiefly in the W. ends. Both square and round heads occur. Several have no rebates. (See Birsay.) St. Ola, Deerness, and perhaps Uya, have no chancels; but all the rest have decided chancels. There is no instance of a chancel door. These have chancel arches equal in width to the chancels.—Orphir, Egilsey, The Ness, Culbinsbrough, Norwick, Kirkaby, and Colvidale. In England this fashion rarely occurs; where it does it is late. It is constructively weak.

Enhallow has a chancel arch, with projecting jambs, of about the English proportion.

Birsay, Wyre, Linton, perhaps Uya, and probably Ness, have or had very narrow chancel arches.

In our early churches the chancels were small in comparison with the naves, and in cathedrals the ritual choir was under the cross or W. of it.

They elongated the choirs in the 13th century, and soon placed the ritual choir E. of the cross.

Orphir and Egilsey had windows with circular heads. Birsay, Wyre, Enhallow, Culbinsbrough, had at least some windows with flat heads. The Ness has all flat. No instance remains of a double light, or of a transom, or a triangular head, which is not unfrequent in Ireland.

At Egilsey, Enhallow, and the Ness are no grooves for glass or rebates, or external chamfers. At Orphir and Birsay are grooves and chamfers. (See account of Egilsey.) Of the 6 churches which retain the E. ends—St. Ola, Orphir, Deerness, Wyre, Egilsey, and the Ness—4 have no E. window, except that in the latter there is a small opening high up in the E. gable. In the early Irish churches it is very unusual not to have an E. window. Probably no apse was without an E. window.

As far as can be made out at present, there was no step to the chancel and no platform for the altar, except the inserted step and altar at Birsay. In some the chancel windows are singularly low, as at Wyre and Egilsey. No piscina remains, and only one sedile, but several ambries.

There are only four cases where we can judge of the pitch of the roofs. The Ness had a roof including about 85 deg., Egilsey about 88 degrees, Enhallow the same, and Wyre about 95 deg. Probably all had rude stepped coping on the gables.

MONUMENTS.

The grave stones found in connection with these churches are of 4 kinds.

1. Keel-shaped slabs placed horizontally on graves as at Sandwick, in Unst, sketched by Mr Irvine.

2. Upright stones nearly rectangular, with crosses engraved on them, as at Sandwick, etched by Mr Irvine, and at Norwick and some other places. This class includes the elaborate monument from Culbinsbrough.

3. The same shaped stones, without any ornamentation, found at many of the old burial grounds.

4. Upright stones cut into the form of crosses, as at Uya.

Mr Irvine has sent the following information :—" I believe from the earliest times in Scotland the foot stone of the grave was the chief stone, and not as now the head stone, and that the E. face of the foot stone was the principal face to be attended to, from the idea that the dead rose at the resurrection to an upright position facing E. Compare the stone with the ancient incised markings from St. Peter's Church, Orkney, now in the Edinburgh Museum, with the one I have etched from Sandwick, Unst, and I believe it will be seen that the keel stone existed to both. Therefore, I believe that the interment belonging to many of the standing stones will be found on the W. side and not on the E." The coffins were often formed of six or more slabs of stone.

PROPORTIONS.

The designs for churches in the ages of architecture were not made at random. Doubtless there existed certain rules of proportion ; but doubtless they varied with times, places, and persons.

Various attempts have been made in modern times to discover these rules, and in some instances with apparent success. It unfortunately happens that we have not often an intact ground plan, and if the original plan was simple, the additions render it complex. In many cases these additions were made without any regard to the proportion of the original.

It appears probable that these proportions were geometric rather than arithmetical —that is to say, made by simple operations of the compasses and rulers, rather than by any proportions of numbers. The small churches of the North are valuable from not having been altered by additions.

Though in the foregoing notes the proportions on which the churches were built may not have been ascertained in all cases, yet in some the coincidences are too remarkable to be chance. Although, no doubt, a system of proportions was extended to the elevations and certain details, yet as to most of these in the churches here enumerated we are in ignorance, because most of the superstructure is gone. It appears that there were, in fact, only 2 figures on which the proportions were founded, a circle, a square, and an equilateral triangle. For most purposes of proportion the circle and square are identical. The "vesica piscis" is 2 equilateral triangles on opposite sides of a common base, and hence equal in proportion to the half of one such triangle.

There is, however, one proportion in which a square is not equivalent to a circle —the diagonal of the square the proportion of which to the side is nearly as 10 to 7. The height or length of an equilateral triangle is to half its base nearly as 7 to 4.

All these proportions are somewhat flexible, inasmuch as they may *include* the side walls and *exclude* the end walls, or the reverse; or they may *include* both, or they may *exclude* both; or they may be applied in one way to the nave, and in another to the chancel, and in another to the tower. But the proportion must not be deemed as ascertained unless the figure really fits within 2 or 3 inches.

DATES.

As to the dates of these buildings, we have but little to guide us. Only fragments of the buildings are left, and those of the plainest description.

Scotch architecture has some mystifying peculiarities. Dates have been suggested from architectural and historical evidence for Orphir, Birsay, and Egilsey. Orphir, 1090—1160; Birsay, 1100; Egilsey, 1000. Wyre has been assigned to the 12th or 13th; the Ness to the 14th, and St. Ola to the 16th century.

It may be fairly observed that there must have been churches erected in the 14th and 15th centuries. Where are the remains of them? Possibly some of those described are of those centuries.

It does not appear impossible that from evidence yet to be collected, a nearer approximation to the dates of these buildings may be got.

APPENDIX B.

The Witch of Howan-Greeny.

(From " The Orcadian," July 21, 1860.)

The early part of the 17th century is noted in the criminal annals of Orkney for numerous trials of persons accused of witchcraft, and the frightful cruelties that were inflicted on these poor victims of superstition by "the law of the land," which is not always in harmony with the law of God. Some of the accusations brought against the alleged witches are extremely ludicrous, while others are painfully suggestive of bitter malice on the part of their authors. The case, however, selected at present to be narrated here, illustrates some of the superstitions most common at the period referred to, and which, to a considerable extent, still exist in the north of Scotland.

Kitty Grieve, or Millar, was a poor widow with a family of several children, and resided in the parish of Evie. Somehow or other she became suspected of witchcraft, and thenceforward was an object of mingled fear and hatred to her neighbours. Repulsed on every hand, and hard pressed by poverty, the poor woman was probably driven in her ignorance and despair to assume the character which had been forced upon her. This supposition will explain her conduct on several occasions when it would otherwise be wholly inexplicable.

At a considerable distance from Kitty's hut, in the direction of the parish of Birsay, there was on the hill-side a hillock known by the name of Howan-Greeny. At the period we refer to, it was covered by the ruins of an old house, and was held to be anything but a "canny" spot to be near after sunset. Even at the present day some of the people in Evie and Birsay considerably quicken their steps, and cast many an uneasy look around them when they have occasion, in the gloaming, to pass the fairy-knowe of Howan-Greeny. "The hill trows," or fairies, are believed yet to linger around the spot, but as in these degenerate days, they are not on the same familiar terms with mortals as in the olden times, their presence is somewhat more feared than courted by those who have still some faith in their existence.

It was on a day in the spring of 1627, that a boy, named James Freshell, who was on the hill near Howan-Greeny, herding the swine of Magnus Smith in Evie, ran for shelter from a heavy shower of cold rain, to the old ruinous house on the knowe. On reaching it, he was greatly surprised to see Kitty Grieve, and his own grandmother, Mary Richart, another reputed witch, and the devil, in the likeness of a black man, sitting between them. So at least ran the story of the boy, whose presence must have been equally unexpected and unwelcome to Kitty, for she immediately called out "fiercely to her black companion to take him, for he would tell upon them." Mary Richart interfered on behalf of her grandson, alleging that nobody would believe what he would say, and so he was allowed to depart unmolested, greatly to the disappointment of Kitty, and on the following morning he told his master what he had seen at Howan-Greeny.

A few months after that occurrence, a woman in Evie, of the name of Ursilla Fea, was one day busily churning milk. It was in the fire-house or "but-end" of a ricketty cottage, whose walls and rafters were richly japanned and festooned by the smoke and soot that went whirling in eddies through the apartment, vainly seeking a sufficient outlet by a hole in the roof, misnamed the "lum" or chimney, through which a few straggling rays of light from the outer world were struggling for admission into the murky interior of the hut. On the middle of the floor were some stones, rudely built in the shape of a low wall about three feet high. In front of this, on a raised hearth, was a huge blazing fire of peats, close to which stood Ursilla, or Osslie, as she was more familiarly addressed, plunging vigorously with her churn-staff in the churn or "kirn," while the perspiration trickled freely down her face ; but the long-looked for butter was not forthcoming. There had she been toiling in vain, hour after hour. Again and again she had returned to the charge, with desperate but unavailing energy. Her task seemed as hopeless and fruitless as if she had been condemned to search for butter on the white foam of the waves which the wild winds churn so fiercely in the caves of Costa Head. As a last resource she heated a large stone, plunged it into the churn, and finally succeeded in getting about two lbs. of butter. This was only about a fourth part of the usual quantity, and Osslie, therefore, in accordance with popular opinion, felt bound to believe that Kitty Grieve, whose character for witchcraft was now fairly established, had "taken away the profit of the milk." The well-known remedy for such a misfortune was immediately resorted to. Osslie's servant was sent off in hot haste to milk the witch's cow, and on her return with the milk it was mixed with that already in the churn, and within a few minutes upwards of 9 lbs. of butter was obtained from the same quantity of milk from which previously all Osslie's "paighing and ploughing" could not extract more than 2 lbs. Osslie, by her own account, paid for her temerity, for in less than 24 hours she was seized with "a deadly disease," which continued to maintain its hold of her for six weeks. At the end of that period Kitty came to Osslie's house and begged a drink out of the churn, saying that if she got it Osslie would be restored to health. The drink was given, Osslie immediately recovered, but the profit of her milk again departed, and up to the date of Kitty's trial no amount of churning had availed to restore it. So ran the testimony of the witnesses.

Kitty was once asked to cure a sick horse, and she recommended the owner to get "three sundry sorts of silver," which he was to put into a sieve, and sift over the back of the horse. Whether this restored him to health or failed to fulfil her promise, we cannot tell.

On another occasion her daughter went, without leave asked or given, and took some cabbages from the yard of John Brown, a farmer in Evie. His servant reproved the girl, who, notwithstanding, took the cabbages home to her mother, to whom she told what occurred. Kitty immediately ordered her daughter to carry back the cabbages, and to cast them at the servant. The latter was struck by them on the chest, and so seriously injured, that she continued ill for a fortnight. Kitty then went to Brown's house and told that she had dreamed that if his wife would give alms to Kitty's daughter, the servant should immediately recover. The alms were given, and forthwith the servant regained her health.

Kitty had also a son, who was a cow-herd to John Brown, who dismissed him from his service. This greatly enraged Kitty, and the consequences to John, as they are narrated in the "Dittay," were not calculated to enlist his sympathies in her behalf, for the dismissal of the boy was immediately followed by the death of one of Brown's cows, and the rest died very shortly afterwards. A similar fate befell the cows of another farmer, who, too, had the ill luck to have a son of Kitty's in his service. In short, Kitty was looked upon as a very dangerous person, who could not be offended with impunity; and, as another instance of this, she was charged at her trial of having gone one morning before sunrise to the house of John Peace, who resided near Kirkwall. She was ordered off by John's wife, who was instantly seized with an extraordinary disease, which rendered her unable to walk from her mother-in-law's house to her own, although the houses were close together, and she had to creep on her hands and knees to her own house. Kitty was sent for, and brought to the bed-side of the sick woman, on whose head she laid her hand, and at the same time gave her a drink of milk, which, it was asserted, she had no sooner done, than the woman recovered the use of her limbs.

There is little doubt that Kitty was driven at last to speak and act as a witch was expected to do; and probably the habit of deceiving others became so inwrought into her nature that she ultimately deceived herself, and believed that she actually possessed the power to which she laid claim. But at all events she acquired great influence over the people by her alternate blessings and imprecations, for the "Dittay" concludes by charging her with "practising witchcrafts, sorceries, divinations, and charms, and giving herself forth to have such craft and knowledge thereby abusing the people, and that by her cursings and imprecations she wronged and hurt man and beast, which evil was brought to pass by the power and working of the devil, her master."

The reputed witch had become so notorious, that she was at last seized, and along with her old companion, Mary Richart, placed in the stocks. While sitting in that uncomfortable position, she reminded Mary of the occurrence at the old house of Howan-Greeny, and bitterly reproached her for shielding on that occasion her grandson, who was now to be brought forward as a witness of what he then saw and heard.

The trial took place before a Sheriff and an assize, in the Wallhouse of the Cathedral of St. Magnus, in Kirkwall, on the 29th day of May, 1633, and the sentence was in the following terms:—"The Judge ordains the pannel to be carried by the lockman (the executioner) to the cross, and burnt on the cheek." Kitty farther became bound, "that if at any time thereafter she should be found to haunt suspected places, or to use charms or the like, she should in that case be burned without dome to death, and that willingly of her own consent." The last clause may be safely enrolled in the extensive category of legal fictions, which often serve most admirably to cover a multitude of other sins.

With such charges against her, Kitty was very fortunate in the comparative leniency of her punishment. In many similar cases the poor creatures accused of witchcraft were sentenced to be strangled, their bodies burnt, and their ashes scattered to the winds of heaven. Probably she owed her escape to the impartiality of the jury, who were chiefly from the parish of St. Ola, and therefore less likely to be influenced by private animosity or local prejudice than persons from the vicinity of Kitty's residence. Her history breaks off abruptly here, leaving no trace of her subsequent career, and no local tradition remains to tell her fate. Whether she was tortured to death amid the jeers and execrations of an enraged and pitiless mob, or was permitted to die in her own humble dwelling, is now unknown. A stray solitary sheet of paper, brown with age, is the only record that has come down to us of the sayings and doings of Kitty Grieve, the once famous witch of Howan-Greeny.

APPENDIX G.
Agricultural Statistics for Orkney and Shetland.

Shewing the Total Acreage under each Kind of Crop, Bare Fallow, and Grass; and No. of Horses, Cattle, Sheep, and Pigs, returned upon 5th June 1883 and 1882.

The Area of Orkney and Shetland together is 612,649 acres.	ORKNEY.		SHETLAND.	
	1883.	1882.	1883.	1882.
	Acres.	*Acres.*	*Acres.*	*Acres.*
Barley or Bere	5,641	6,026	2,478	2,610
Oats	32,781	32,330	8,050	8,123
Rye	1			
Beans	2	1	—	—
Peas	34	26	—	—
Total of Corn Crops	38,459	38,383	10,528	10,733
Green Crops:—				
Potatoes	3,104	3,221	3,357	3,313
Turnips and Swedes	14,387	14,164	943	869
Mangold				
Carrots			—	—
Cabbage, Kohl-Rabi, and Rape	56	57	211	197
Vetches and other Green Crops, except Clover or Grass	305	297	—	2
Total of Green Crops	17,852	17,739	4,511	4,381
Clover, Sanfoin, and Grasses under Rotation	32,051	31,646	780	761
Permanent Pasture or Grass not broken up in Rotation (exclusive of Heath or Mountain Land)	22,755	21,686	41,628	41,686
Flax				
Hops				
Bare Fallow or Uncropped Arable Land	1,031	1,143	946	928
Horses (including Ponies), as returned by occupiers of land:—				
Used solely for purpose of Agriculture, &c.	4,884	4,949	908	932
Unbroken Horses and Mares kept solely for Breeding	1,208	1,167	4,397	4,338
Total of Horses	6,092	6,116	5,305	5,270
Cattle:—				
Cows and Heifers in Milk or in Calf	9,405	9,386	8,132	8,712
Other Cattle—2 Years of Age and above	3,621	3,755	6,314	5,852
Under 2 Years of Age	12,598	12,742	6,899	5,531
Total of Cattle	25,624	25,883	21,345	20,095
Sheep:—				
1 Year old and above	17,337	16,484	50,171	50,712
Under 1 Year Old	14,211	13,943	30,992	28,591
Total of Sheep	31,548	30,427	81,163	79,303
Pigs	4,745	4,862	3,788	3,749

APPENDIX D.

Kirkwall Town House.

The Town Council of Kirkwall having resolved to erect a new Town House and Tolbooth, applied to the Earl of Morton, then in possession of the earldon of Orkney, to aid them. On 2nd June, 1740, Bailie Groat communicated to the Council that Lord Morton "had made a compliment to the Burgh of £200, to be laid out by the Magistrates and Council towards building a new Tolbooth in the town, and the Provost was desired to return thanks to the Earl," and to intimate that the £200 would be laid out in "good hands upon interest until the town laid themselves out for materials for building said Tolbooth, and also for making up a greater sum for that work." On 7th September, 1742, the Magistrates and Council wrote to the Earl of Morton for liberty to use some of the stones of the old Castle of Kirkwall, and received the following answer :—

"Aberdour, October 14th 1742.

"GENTLEMEN,—I Received your Letter of the 7th Septr., Desiring the Liberty of Some of the Stones out of the Old Castle of Kirkwall for building your Town house. I am very willing to Comply wt. your Request, But I expect yt. in consideration of my former Donation to the Town for that purpose and of this present allowanc to take some of those Stones, That you will therefore by an Act of your Town Council Declare the principall Hall in this intended Building to belong Equally to the Sherieff for keeping his Courts as to the Magestrates and Council for holding theirs ; I am the more particular in mentioning this Condition at present, Because I've been told that some Scruples were raised against allowing the Sherieff to have any right in that Building, Tho' if any of the Gentlemen who were present when I declared my intention of making this Donation in the Court of Justiciary will recollect they must Remember that I then said I gave yt. Sum to Build a Room for keeping Courts and a Sufficient Prison in the Town of Kirkwall, That the Majestrates might not be under a necessity of using Such means to Secure their prisoners as Carried any appearance of Hardships or Cruelty.

"Wishing Prosperity to the Good Town, and to yourselves in Particular I remain, —Gentlemen your most obedt. Humble servt., MORTON."

The Council held several meetings in November following, to consider the terms and conditions contained in Lord Morton's letter, and on the 16th November, 1742, they finally passed a resolution in accordance with the terms of his Lordship's letter, giving "the right, use, and privilege of the principal or common hall of the Town House intended to be built, for the keeping and holding of Stewart, Sheriff, and Justiciary Courts therein at pleasure by the Sheriffs, their Deputes and Substitutes, with the special provision and condition that in case these Courts shall at any time happen to fall upon one and the same day with the Town Courts or Councils of this Burgh, that the said Town Courts or Council in that case shall have the preference, declaring always that the Magistrates for the time being by themselves or their servants shall have the sole keeping of the keys of said Tolbooth and Prison House intended to be built and whole rooms and apartments thereof."

APPENDIX E.

Bells of St Magnus.

(BY SIR HENRY DRYDEN, BART.)

There are four bells in St Magnus—
1. (largest) originally given by Bishop Maxwell, but recast.
2. Given by Bishop Maxwell.
3. The same.
4. (smallest) without inscription or date, not hung.

They are not, and probably never have been, rung by the common processes of wheel or crank, but by a rope applied so as, by a nearly lateral traction, to make the tongue strike the side. One end of a short rope is fastened to the tongue and the other to the wall; a second rope is fastened to the middle of the first (T), and the lower end of it pulled by the ringer (Y), which of course pulls the tongue to one side.

The notes produced by the bells are not at diatonic intervals, being about five quarter-tones apart. They are about G ¼ tone sharp, A ½ tone sharp, C¼ tone sharp.

The second bell is used for the clock, and is struck by the clock-hammer on the *outside*, giving, when so struck, a note lower than that given when struck by the tongue.

FIRST BELL.—Note—tenor G ¼ tone sharp; 3 feet 5½ inches diameter, and 2 feet 9 inches high, exclusive of the crown. Inscription in plain capitals, raised, in two lines :—

> "Made by master Robbert Maxvell, Bischop of Orkney, the yeer of God MDXXVIII, the year of the reign of King James the V. Robert Borthwik made mein the castel of Edinburgh."

In an oval medallion—

> "Taken et brought againe heir by Alexander Geddus, marchant in Kirkwa, and recasten at Amsterdam, Jully 1682 years, by Cladius Fremy, city bell caster. It weighs 1450 P.

On a medallion a figure with a sword, and under it SCT MAGNVS,

On a raised shield the arms of Bishop Maxwell—a saltier with annulet in centre.

Bishop Maxwell was the son of Sir John Maxwell of Pollock, Co. Renfrew, and had for his arms *Argent*, saltier *sable*, with annulet *or* in the centre, maternal difference for Eglintoun.

In August 1682 "the great bell" being "rift" was sent "to Amsterdam to be re-cast." The Bishop of Orkney and Magistrates of Kirkwall gave instructions to the person to whose care the bell was entrusted, that "there be ane special and diligent care had that the letters already about the bell be again re-formed as the samin is conform to ane note thereof sent with it, together with the several arms already thereupon, viz., the arms of Scotland, being ane Lyon within the Shield, with the portrait of Sainct Magnus, and the Maxwells arms, and that the samin be placed upon the said bell as the samin is at present. That there be added thereto, underneath the said letters and arms, this line, viz:— 'This bell recasten at   for Kirkwall, in anno 1682.' And to mark the weight thereof on the bell."

The old bell on being weighed at Amsterdam was found to be 1500 lbs. It lost in casting, 165 lbs. To which was added of new metal, 198 lbs.

Weight of new bell   .   .   .   1528 lbs.

do. of new tongue,   . .   46

Total,   1574

The whole cost was 1303 merks Scots,—about £72 7s 9½d sterling.

The weight marked on the bell does not agree with this statement; nor did the caster follow the directions to recast the letters as they were before.

SECOND BELL.—Note—A ½ tone sharp; 3 feet 1 inch diameter; and 2 feet 5 inches high exclusive of crown. Inscription in black letter, capitals and small, raised, in two lines :—

> "Maid be maister robert maxvell, bischop of Orknay, in ye secund yier of his
>
>   m c
>
> consecration in the zeir of god I V XXVIII. zeiris ye XV. zeir of ye reign
>
> King James V.

On a medallion a figure with a sword, and under it "Sanctus Magnus."

Below—"robert borthvik." On a medallion the arms of Scotland, and on another the arms of Maxwell as before.

THIRD BELL.—Note—middle C ¼ tone sharp ; 2 feet 9 inches diameter, and 2 feet 5 inches high, exclusive of crown. Inscription in black letter, capitals and small, raised, in three lines :—

"Maid be maister robert maxvel, byschop of Orknay, ye secund zier of his
m c
consecration ye zier of gode I V XXVIII zeris ye XV. zier of Kyng

James ye V. be robert borthvyk maid al thre in ye castel of Edynburgh."

On a medallion a figure of St Magnus.
On a shield the arms of Maxwell as before.
FOURTH BELL.—Not hung ; 1 foot 8 inches diameter, and 1 foot 4 inches high, exclusive of crown. No inscription. It is called "the fire bell," and in the 17th century was called "the skellat bell."

APPENDIX F.

Fishing Lochs and Streams.

LOCH BEA.—A small loch, in the parish of Cross, Island of Sanday. It is open to the public, and yields good eel fishing.

LOCH GRÆMESHALL is about 5 miles from Kirkwall, belonging to Mr Græme, of Græmeshall, who is very kind in granting leave to fish. It contains small trout, 3 or 4 to a lb., but sport is very uncertain. The best bait is worm, but towards August fly sometimes does well.

LOCH HUNDLAND.—A loch about a mile by half a mile, situated between Loch Swannay and Twatt. The Kirbuster Burn flows out of it. It is open to the public. The trout in it run 2 or 3 to a lb., and 12 lbs. may be killed on a good day from April to September with a red or black hackle.

LOCH ISBISTER is in the parish of Rendall, and belongs to Dr Logie and Mrs Robertson. It is not exactly open to the public, but leave is not very difficult to obtain. The loch contains excellent sea-trout, and good sport is often got. Some of the trout weigh 5 lb. each. The best time is from July to October.

LOCH KIRBUSTER.—In the parish of Orphir. It is 1½ miles long by half a mile broad, and is open to the public. There are good trout in it, and during September and October sea-trout go up in considerable numbers. The common loch trout are 2 or 3 to a lb., and the sea-trout are of good weights. Dark brown flies are the best.

LOCH ST. MARY'S is in the parish of Holm, to which the description of Loch Græmeshall will apply, save that here there are sea-trout in addition.

LOCH SAVISKAIL is in the island of Rousay. It is the best of all the Rousay lochs, of which there are six, some larger and some smaller than this one, but not yielding such good sport. They are called the "Peerie" Lochs or little lochs. Saviskail belongs to General Traill Burroughs, of Rousay, and leave must be got from him or his factor. The "Roost" or race tide, a sort of extended Maelstrom, lies between Rousay and the mainland of Orkney. There are yellow trout (some of them of great weight) in Loch Saviskail, but the average size is ½ lb. or so. The best time is May to the end of September.

LOCH STENNIS is the chief of the Orkney lochs, and is about 9 miles by 1½ at its greatest breadth. The principal proprietors are Col. Balfour, of Balfour Castle, and Mr W. G. T. Watt, Kierfiold House. There are boats, of which strangers may sometimes get the use, and the loch is mostly open to the public. It contains abundance of sea-trout, and capital baskets are often made, especially with worm. June, July, August, and September are the best months ; in September the sport is best, and the fish in fine condition.

LOCH SWANNAY OR SWONA.—A loch about one mile long by half a mile broad, in the parish of Birsay. Mr Brotchie, of Swannay, is the proprietor. It holds a great number of trout, some of them very large. Ordinary flies are used, but the angler in Orkney should always have a good supply of worm. From May to the end of September is the best time.

LOCH SAINTEAR.—A little loch having a few trout, in the parish of Westray. Above it is another small lake, Burness, which flows into Saintear, and both fall into the bay of Pierowall. Sea-trout go up in September and October, and are sometimes caught in the little stream which joins them to the sea.

LOCH TREDWALL.—An exceedingly pretty lake in Papa—parish of Westray. It stretches almost across the island, in a south-westerly direction, and has in the centre, on a charming little islet, the ruins of a chapel dedicated to St. Tredwall, a female saint. The whole island in which it is situated is the property of Mr Traill of Holland, Kirkwall, from whom leave to fish must be obtained, but sport is not very great.

LOCH TWATT OR KIRBUSTER, OR BOARDHOUSE, OR BIRSAY.—A loch about two miles long in the parish of Birsay. It belongs to the Earl of Zetland, and is open to the public. The loch contains trout (there are no salmon in Orkney), and many of them are several lbs. weight. The best time is from May to the beginning of October, and capital sport is often to be had.

LOCHS AND STREAMS OF WALLS AND HOY.—If we include mountain tarns, there must be some hundreds of lochs in these parishes, but all are of small size, except three in Walls, named Heldale's or Helial's Water, Hoglin's Water, and Sands Water. Both the former lochs are deep, over 12 fathoms; but the former—Heldale's Water—which is nearly two miles long, alone contains fish. About 30 years ago *char* were found to exist in this lake, said to have been introduced from Norway by an ancestor of the present proprietor. They run from $\frac{1}{4}$ lb. to 3 lbs., averaging $\frac{3}{4}$ lb.; but rarely take fly or bait. Some *S. Fario* and *S. Levenensis* from Howietoun were placed in the lake a few seasons ago, but numbers died in transit, and it is not yet known if many survived. We understand the char in this lake is considered a variety more approaching to those of Norway than to any British char. With the exception of a shallow piece of water in Hoy used as a mill-dam, which holds some small trout, all the other lochs are void of fish. There are several streams containing the usual little dark fish, probably chiefly the young of the sea-trout, which rarely run up to $\frac{1}{4}$ lb. The largest burns are at Rackwick, Hoy, and Mill Bay, and Oar Bay, Walls. At the beginning of the close season a considerable number of sea-trout seek these streams to spawn, and formerly were much "netted" at remote streams, regardless of their condition. At other seasons it is very uncommon to find the sea-trout in any of the streams, as unfortunately those from the larger lochs fall over precipices inaccessible to fish. Salmon occasionally frequent the stream at Rackwick, and other points in Hoy, and the proprietor has the fishings in his charters. All the above lochs and streams are on the property of Mr J. G. Moodie Heddle of Melsetter, and cannot be fished without leave from him. Leave to fish may usually be obtained for any place not let along with shootings, by making application in writing a few days beforehand Mr Moodie Heddle is always willing to put naturalists in the way of getting information or specimens, if they will apply to him direct, and avoid encouraging people to rob the nests of the rarer birds, and do other damage. Offers of high prices for eggs have exterminated the eagles, and very nearly, a few years since, several other birds. Seals would have been extinct in South Isles probably, had they not been protected and allowed to breed, near Melsetter, for some years.

LOCH WASDALE, in the parish of Firth, and belonging to the trustees of the late Mr Scarth, of Binscarth. It is well stocked with trout. Permission to angle must be obtained.

There are numerous little streams containing excellent fish, especially in August September, and October, when the sea-trout come up in great numbers. The angler will, as a rule, find the best sport in the estuaries, unless he has the ill-fortune to arrive immediately after they have been cleaned by nets which frequently land beautiful trout in abundance. The principal streams are :—

The Wideford, near Kirkwall, a shallow burn, containing a small delicately-avoured trout. Good sport in the sea at its mouth during the summer and autumn months.

The Burns of Toab and Sebay, in St. Andrew's parish, have common brown and sea-trout in considerable numbers.

The Holm Burn falls into the Loch of Græmeshall and has only small fish.

The Rossmire, in Firth parish, usually abounding in trout.

The Orphir Burn, in Orphir parish, one of the best in Orkney.

The Berridale, in Hoy parish, with a few stunted indigenous trees on its banks.

The Trumbland, in Rousay parish and island, more frequented by the botanist than by the angler

The Burns of Swannay, Kirbister, and Birsay, in Birsay parish, are all condered good.

There are many other small streams in all parts of the islands, where the angler can fill his basket, if he has been disappointed both on the lochs and in the estuaries.

APPENDIX G.

Orkney Nick-names.

Kirkwall—"Starlings."
St. Andrews—"Skerry Scrapers."
Deerness—"Skate Rumples."
Holm—"Hobblers."
Orphir—"Yearnings."
Firth—"Oysters."
Stromness—"Bloody Puddings."
Sandwick—"Ash Patties."
Harray—"Crabs."
Birsay—"Dogs" or "Hoes."
Evie—"Cauld Kail."
Rendall—"Sheep Thieves."
Hoy—"Hawks."
Walls—"Lyres."
Burray—"Oily Bogies."
South Ronaldsay:—Grimness—"Gruties;" Hope—"Scouties;" Widewall—"Witches;" Herston—"Hogs;" Sandwick—"Birkies;" South Parish—"Teeacks."
Gairsay—"Buckies."
Veira or Wyre—"Whelks."
Egilsay—"Burstin-lumps."
Rousay—"Mares."
Shapinsay—"Sheep."
Stronsay—"Limpets."
Sanday—"Gruellie Belkies."
North Ronaldshay—"Seals," "Hides," or "Hoydes."
Eday—"Scarfs."
Westray—"Auks."
Papa Westray—"Dundies."

THE END.

KIRKWALL: PRINTED BY JAMES ANDERSON, "ORCADIAN" OFFICE.

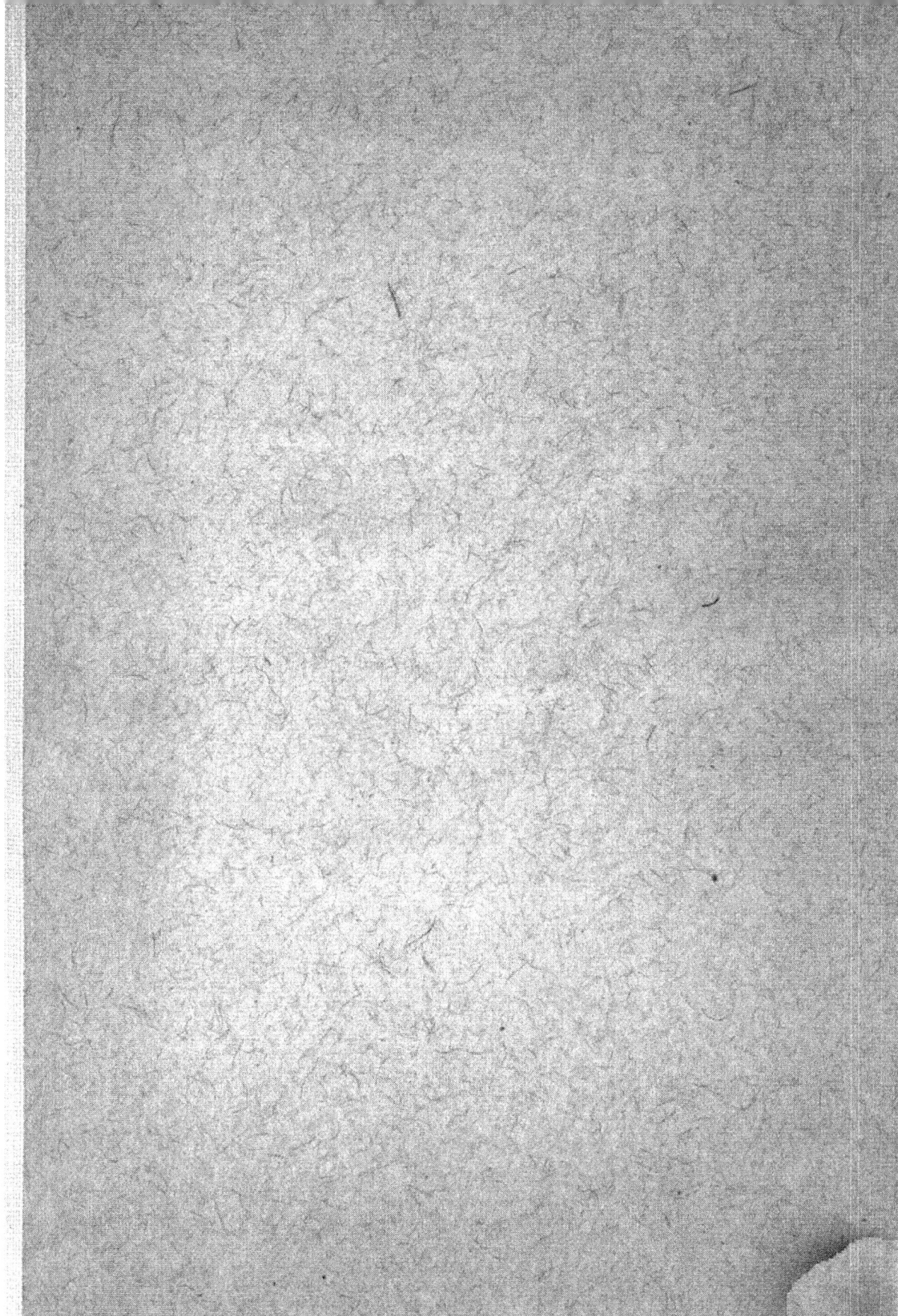

CPSIA information can be obtained at www.ICGtesting.com
Printed in the USA
BVOW08s2053051214

378129BV00020B/555/P

9 781179 847436